THE BUSINESS BLOCKCHAIN

THE BUSINESS
BLOCKCHAIN

Promise, Practice, and Application of
the Next Internet Technology

WILLIAM MOUGAYAR

FOREWORD BY VITALIK BUTERIN

For my parents, who
continue to be by my side.

To Maureen, with whom
everything is possible.

And to our beloved dog, Pasha,
the brave little Bichon Frisé.
You filled my heart forever.

CONTENTS

FOREWORD

THIS DECADE IS AN INTERESTING TIME for the development of decentralized technologies. Although cryptographers, mathematicians and coders have been working on increasingly specific and advanced protocols in order to get stronger and stronger privacy and authenticity guarantees out of various systems—from electronic cash to voting to file transfer—progress was slow for over 30 years. The innovation of the blockchain—or, more generally, the innovation of public economic consensus by Satoshi Nakamoto in 2009—proved to be the one missing piece of the puzzle that single-handedly gave the industry its next giant leap forward.

The political environment seemed to almost snap into place: the great financial crisis in 2008 spurred growing distrust in mainstream finance, including both corporations and the governments that are normally supposed to regulate them, and was the initial spark that drove many to seek out alternatives. Then Edward Snowden's revelations in 2013, highlighting how active the government was in realms citizens once believed private, were the icing on the cake. Even though blockchain technologies specifically have not seen mainstream adoption as a result, the underlying spirit of decentralization to a substantial degree has.

Applications ranging from Apple's phones to WhatsApp have started building in forms of encryption that are so strong that even the company writing the software and managing the servers cannot break it. For those who prefer corporations to government as their boogeyman of choice, the advent of "sharing economy 1.0" is increasingly showing signs of failure to fulfill what many had originally seen to be its promise. Rather than simply cutting out entrenched and oligopolistic intermediaries, giants like Uber are simply replacing the middleman with themselves, and not always doing a better job of it.

Blockchains, and the umbrella of related technologies that I have collectively come to call "crypto 2.0," provide an attractive fix. Rather than simply hoping that the parties we interact with behave honorably, we are building technological systems that inherently build the desired properties into the system, in such a way that they will keep functioning with the guarantees that we expect, even if many of the actors involved are corrupt.

All transactions under "crypto 2.0" come with auditable trails of cryptographic proofs. Decentralized peer-to-peer networks can be used to reduce reliance on any single server; public key cryptography could create a notion of portable user-controlled identities. More advanced kinds of math, including ring signatures, homomorphic encryption, and zero-knowledge proofs, guarantee privacy, allowing users to put all of their data in the open in such a way that certain properties of it can be verified, and even computed on, without actually revealing any private details.

What is most surprising to early adopters of the technology, however, is just how rapidly institutional adoption has spread in the last two years. All the way from 2011 to 2013, the blockchain scene—or, realistically, what was then just the "bitcoin" scene— was very cryptoanarchist in spirit, with colorful and idealistic revolutionaries excited about "fighting the power" (or, more precisely, routing around the power). Today in 2016, however, the most exciting announcements all have to do with some collaboration announced with IBM or Microsoft, a research paper by the Bank of England, or a banking consortium announcing yet another round of new members.

What happened? In part, I would argue that the cryptoanarchists underestimated how flexible, technologically progressive, and even idealistic large corporations and banks can be. We often forget that corporations are made up of people, and people inside of corporations often have similar values and concerns to the kinds of regular people whom you might find at meetups. It might seem as though "the trust machine," as *The Economist* calls it, is purely a replacement for centralized anchors of trust, both in finance and elsewhere, that rely on real-world reputation and regulatory oversight, but the reality is much more complex. In truth, institutions do not fully trust one another either, and centralized institutions in one industry are just as concerned about centralization in other industries as regular people are. Energy companies, which are involved in producing and selling electricity, are just as happy to sell to a decentralized market as they are to a centralized one, and they may even prefer the decentralized version if it takes a smaller cut.

Furthermore, many industries are decentralized already, to an extent that many people outside of these industries do not appreciate, but they are decentralized in an inefficient way—a way that requires each company to maintain its own infrastructure around managing users, transactions, and data, and to reconcile with the systems of other companies every time it needs to interact. Consolidation around a single market leader would, in fact, make these industries more efficient. But neither the competitors of the likely leader nor antitrust regulators are willing to accept that outcome, leading to a stalemate. Until now. With the advent of decentralized databases that can technologically replicate the network effect gains of a single monopoly, everyone can join and align for their benefit, without actually creating a monopoly with all the negative consequences that it brings.

This is the story that arguably drives the interest in consortium chains in finance, blockchain applications in the supply chain industry, and blockchain-based identity systems. They all use decentralized databases to replicate the gains of everyone being on one platform without the costs of having to agree on who gets to control that platform and then put up with them if they choose to try to abuse their monopoly position.

In the first four years after Satoshi's launch of Bitcoin in January 2009, much attention focused on the currency, including its payment aspects and its function as an alternative store of value. In 2013, attention started to shift to the "blockchain 2.0" applications: uses of the same technology that underlies Bitcoin's decentralization and security to other applications, ranging from domain name registration to financial contracts to crowdfunding and even games. The core insight behind my own platform, Ethereum, was that a Turing-complete programming language, embedded into the protocol at the base layer, could be used as the ultimate abstraction, allowing developers to build applications with any kind of business logic or purpose while benefiting from the blockchain's core properties. Around the same time, systems such as the decentralized storage platform InterPlanetary File System (IPFS) began to emerge, and cryptographers came out with powerful new tools that could be used in combination with blockchain technology to add privacy, particularly zk-SNARKs, or zero-knowledge Succinct Non-Interactive ARgument Knowledge. The combination of Turing-complete blockchain computing, non-blockchain decentralized networks using similar cryptographic technologies, and the integration of blockchains with advanced cryptography was what I chose to call "crypto 2.0"—a title that may be ambitious, but which I feel best captures the spirit of the movement in its widest form.

What is crypto 3.0? In part, the continuation of some of the trends in crypto 2.0, and particularly generalized protocols that provide both computational abstraction and privacy. But equally important is the current technological elephant in the room in the blockchain sphere: scalability. Currently, all existing blockchain protocols have the property that every computer in the network must process every transaction—a property that provides extreme degrees of fault tolerance and security, but at the cost of ensuring that the network's processing power is effectively bounded by the processing power of a single node.

Crypto 3.0—at least in my mind—consists of approaches that move beyond this limitation, in one of various ways to create systems that break through this limitation and actually achieve the scale needed to support mainstream adoption (technically astute readers may have heard of "lightning networks," "state channels," and "sharding").

And then, there is also the question of adoption. Aside from the simple currency use case, "crypto 2.0" in 2015 saw a lot of people talking about it, developers releasing base platforms, but not yet any substantial applications. In 2016, we are seeing both startups and institutional players develop proof of concepts. Of course, the vast majority of these will never get anywhere and slowly wither away and die. That is inevitable in any field. It is a truism of entrepreneurship generally that 90% of all new businesses fail. But the 10% that succeed will likely at some point be scaled up into full-on products that reach millions of people—and that's where the fun really begins.

Perhaps William's book will inspire you to understand and, perhaps, join in refining the business blockchain.

Vitalik Buterin

Ethereum inventor and Chief Scientist,
Ethereum Foundation

APRIL 2, 2016

ACKNOWLEDGMENTS

SOME SAY WRITING A BOOK is a labor of love, and they are right. For me, it felt like assembling a puzzle on a canvas, then framing it.

Book writing is like an act of gift exchanging. The author spends an enormous amount of time to organize and concentrate their thoughts in writing. In return, readers donate their valuable time. Sometimes, a relationship develops between the author and readers. In my case, I welcome any reader who wishes to email me at wmougayar@gmail.com.

The moment I became involved in the blockchain industry, several people contributed to the shaping of my thinking and insights, but no single person had more influence on my education than Vitalik Buterin, creator and Chief Scientist at Ethereum. I am forever indebted to his time and knowledge, which he shared generously.

To all the creators, innovators, pioneers, leaders, entrepreneurs, startups, enterprise executives and practitioners who are living at the leading edges of this technological revolution, thank you for helping me connect the dots. You are the ones shining the lights ahead, despite some early pockets of darkness. My interactions with you have been invaluable. Thank you for allowing me a front seat, or backstage access to your wonderful acts.

At the risk of leaving some unnamed individuals in my professional circles, I would like to extend a very special gratitude to Muneeb Ali, Ian Allison,* Juan Benet, Pascal Bouvier,* Chris Allen, Jerry Brito, Anthony Di Iorio, Leda Glyptis, Brian Hoffman,* Andrew

Those indicated by asterik (*) were kind enough to review portions of the final manuscript.

Keys, Juan Llanos, Joseph Lubin, Adam Ludwin, Joel Monegro, Chris Owen, Sam Patterson, Denis Nazarov, Rodolfo Novak, Michael Perklin, Robert Sams,* Washington Sanchez, Amber Scott, Ryan Selkis, Barry Silbert, Ryan Shea, Ageesen Sri, Nick Sullivan, Nick Szabo, Tim Swanson, Simon Taylor,* Wayne Vaughan, Jesse Walden, Albert Wenger, Jeffrey Wilcke, Fred Wilson, and Gavin Wood. They all contributed, in different ways, to my understanding of Bitcoin, cryptocurrencies, blockchains, and their (decentralized) applications, either by teaching me, showing me, debating me, or allowing me into a piece of their world where I learned.

Special thanks to Wiley executive editor Bill Falloon, who believed we could do this faster than humanly possible, and to Kevin Barrett Kane at The Frontispiece who designed and produced the book in the nick of time.

Finally, much appreciation to the group of friends who helped support this book's Kickstarter campaign in February 2016, which made its production feasible. I could not have done this without you, and without the support of Margot Atwell and John Dimatos from Kickstarter.

One of a kind, Most Generous Supporter: Brad Feld (Foundry Group).

Really GENEROUS Supporters: Jim Orlando (OMERS Ventures), Ryan Selkis (DCG), Matthew Spoke (Deloitte).

Super SPECIAL Supporters: Kevin Magee, Piet Van Overbeke, Christian Gheorghe, Jon Bradford.

Super BIG Supporters: David Cohen (Techstars), Matthew Roszak (Bloq), Mark Templeton, Duncan Logan (RocketSpace), Michael Dalesandro.

BIG Supporters: Ahmed Alshaia, Floyd DCosta, Heino Døssing, Larry Erlich, Felix Frei, Jay Grieves, Emiel van der Hoek, Fergus Lemon, Amir Moulavi, Daniel A Greenspun, Michael O'Loughlin, Narry Singh, Amar Varma, Donna Brewington White, Neil Warren, Albert Wenger.

A PERSONAL PREFACE

I HAVE NOT ALWAYS BEEN SO LUCKY IN MANY THINGS, but one thing I lucked out on was my initial encounter with Vitalik Buterin, Ethereum's principal inventor who happened to be living in the same city as I did: Toronto.

On a cold early January 2014 evening, Vitalik came down the stairs at Bitcoin Decentral in an old narrow building on Spadina Avenue, an hour prior to the start of one of the weekly Toronto Bitcoin Meetups, organized by Anthony Di Iorio. I spoke to him for the first time, trying to understand something that was described to me, as "beyond Bitcoin." For six months prior to that, I had been trying to understand Bitcoin, and this Ethereum technology was news to me.

Soon after my conversation started, the room was filling with people entering the building, ready for the Meetup to start. There was a special buzz around because Vitalik had just published his white paper[1] on a new blockchain platform that was supposed to be better than Bitcoin, and destined to become the next big thing.

Curious and intrigued, I proceeded to bombard Vitalik with questions about Ethereum and its architecture. I was impressed by his invention, but I was more interested in how it was going to be deployed. Vitalik didn't have all the answers. But he radiated a contagiously positive (yet slightly naive, at the time) determination and optimism about a better world out there. I sensed that this wasn't just about technology. It was more profound. It was about society, government, business, old and new beliefs. It was about all of us. There was a human element to this technology that proposed more equitable solutions to our already complex and unjust world.

Two weeks later, I sat down with Vitalik and almost forced him to draw up an architecture of how Ethereum would work in the context of a deployment framework. I created my own hand drawn primitive version and showed it to him. He looked at it for three seconds, got agitated, opened Inkscape on his Windows PC, and frenetically started drawing the first version of a blockchain-based architectural framework with Ethereum in it. That architecture drawing was later iterated upon, and appeared in one of Vitalik's blog posts, titled "On Silos."[2]

Over the next several months, and up to this day, we became reverse mentors. He taught me a lot about blockchains, and I advised him on business matters and growing Ethereum. I may never comprehend a fraction of Vitalik's blockchain dreams on a given night, but one thing I am certain about, is that Vitalik Buterin is emerging as a savvy business person, following the ranks of other bright technologists, while continuing to lead the Ethereum core technology and its Foundation.

I proceeded to write 50 blog posts on Bitcoin, blockchains, and Ethereum, and immersed myself with global creators, innovators, pioneers, leaders, entrepreneurs, startups, enterprise executives and practitioners who were at the leading edges of blockchain technology and its implementation.

Much of this book is marked by the historical perspective I hold, which is based on 34 years of experience in the technology sector. The first phase of this journey included 14 formative years at Hewlett-Packard, followed by a second phase of 10 years as an independent consultant, author and influencer in the Internet space (1995–2005). In 1996, I authored one of the first business books on Internet business strategy, *Opening Digital Markets*, allowing me to exhaustively analyze the significance of the Web on business, and work with small and large companies who were implementing it. In 2005, I learned how to become a professional analyst at Aberdeen Group, then followed that stint by three years at Cognizant Technology Solutions, where I became exposed to the true meanings of a borderless organization, with global arbitrage at the center of it. In 2008, and for another five years, I dived into the startup world as a founder of two mildly successful startups (Eqentia, and Engagio). They say you learn as much from failures as from successes.

My passion for the blockchain's peer-to-peer (P2P) technology was not a coincidence. In 2001, I had launched PeerIntelligence. com, a site that chronicled the first wave of P2P technologies. During this time, P2P was primarily about file sharing, and I gained an early appreciation of the power of this new technology. Sadly, these first attempts at P2P died on the vine, after legal assaults killed Napster, but in return, we gained the BitTorrent protocol as its valiant remnant.

All these experiences helped shape my thoughts about the blockchain, and influenced the preparation of this book.

In 2013, when I discovered Bitcoin and the world of blockchains, it brought me back to the early excitement of 1995, when some of us knew that the Internet was going to be transformational, coupled with flash backs about the early P2P days of 2001. Luckily, P2P was getting a shot in the arm in 2009 when the Bitcoin blockchain took its first breath.

When I was first exposed to the blockchain, I was reminded of Andy Grove's words in his 1996 book, *Only the Paranoid Survive*. He wrote, *"There's wind and then there's a typhoon. In this business you always have winds. But a 10x force is a change in an element of one's business of typhoon force."* Of course, Andy was talking about the Internet, as a typhoon force that fundamentally alters one's business. Today, the blockchain is that 10x typhoon force that is going to alter many businesses, and the journey is just starting.

I will admit that I went through great pains trying to understand the many facets of the blockchain. Many of its smart visionaries were technically inclined people who didn't focus on succinctly explaining its business implications, or intersections. My early quest to understand the blockchain required a lot of teeth pulling and tea leaves reading to connect the dots and find clarity. It was an agonizing encounter, and the source of my impetus for writing this book. I was determined to make it less dreadful for the rest of us to understand this technology and its ramifications.

The blockchain is part of the history of the Internet. It is at the same level as the World Wide Web in terms of importance, and arguably might give us back the Internet, in the way it was supposed to be: more decentralized, more open, more secure, more private, more equitable, and more accessible. Ironically, many blockchain applications also have a shot at replacing legacy Web applications, at the same time as they will replace legacy businesses that cannot loosen their grips on heavy-handed centrally enforced trust functions.

No matter how it unfolds, the blockchain's history will continue to be written well after you finish reading this book, just as the history of the Web continued to be written well after its initial invention. But here's what will make the blockchain's future even more interesting: you are part of it.

I hope that readers will find *The Business Blockchain* as useful as I found it exhilarating to write.

William Mougayar
Toronto, Ontario
wmougayar@gmail.com

MARCH 2016

NOTES

1. "A Next-Generation Smart Contract and Decentralized Application Platform," https://github.com/ethereum/wiki/wiki/White-Paper#ethereum.

2. "On Silos," https://blog.ethereum.org/2014/12/31/silos/.

INTRODUCTION

IF THE BLOCKCHAIN has not shocked you yet, I guarantee it will shake you soon.

I have not seen anything like this since the start of the Internet, in terms of capturing the imagination of people, a small number first, but then spreading rapidly.

Welcome to the new world of the blockchain and blockchains.

At its core, the blockchain is a technology that permanently records transactions in a way that cannot be later erased but can only be sequentially updated, in essence keeping a never-ending historical trail. This seemingly simple functional description has gargantuan implications. It is making us rethink the old ways of creating transactions, storing data, and moving assets, and that's only the beginning.

The blockchain cannot be described just as a revolution. It is a marching phenomenon, slowly advancing like a tsunami, and gradually enveloping everything along its way by the force of its progression. Plainly, it is the second significant overlay on top of the Internet, just as the Web was that first layer back in 1990. That new layer is mostly about trust, so we could call it the *trust layer*.

Blockchains are enormous catalysts for change that hit at governance, ways of life, traditional corporate models, society and global institutions. Blockchain infiltration will be met with resistance, because it is an extreme change.

Blockchains defy old ideas that are locked in our minds for

decades, if not centuries. Blockchains will challenge governance and centrally controlled ways of enforcing transactions. For example, why pay an escrow to clear a title insurance if the blockchain can automatically check it in an irrefutable way?

Blockchains loosen up trust, which has been in the hands of central institutions (e.g., banks, policy makers, clearinghouses, governments, large corporations), and allows it to evade these old control points. For example, what if counterparty validation can be done on the blockchain, instead of by a clearinghouse?

An analogy would be when, in the 16th century, medieval guilds helped to maintain monopolies on certain crafts against outsiders, by controlling the printing of knowledge that would explain how to copy their work. They accomplished that type of censorship by being in cahoots with the Catholic Church and governments in most European countries that regulated and controlled printing by requiring licenses. That type of central control and monopoly didn't last too long, and soon enough, knowledge was free to travel after an explosion in printing. To think of printing knowledge as an illegal activity would be unfathomable today. We could think of the traditional holders of central trust as today's guilds, and we could question why they should continue holding that trust, if technology (the blockchain) performed that function as well or even better.

Blockchains liberate the trust function from outside existing boundaries, in the same way as medieval institutions were forced to cede control of printing.

It is deceptive to view the blockchain primarily as a distributed ledger, because it represents only one of its many dimensions. It's like describing the Internet as a network only, or as just a publishing platform. These are necessary but not sufficient conditions or properties; blockchains are also greater than the sum of their parts.

Blockchain proponents believe that trust should be free, and not in the hands of central forces that tax it, or control it in one form or another (e.g., fees, access rights, or permissions). They believe that trust can be and should be part of peer-to-peer relationships, facilitated by technology that can enforce it. Trust can be coded up, and it can be computed to be true or false by way of mathematically-backed certainty, that is enforced by powerful encryption to cement it. In essence, trust is replaced by cryptographic proofs, and trust is maintained by a network of trusted computers (honest nodes) that ensure its security, as contrasted with single entities who create overhead or unnecessary bureaucracy around it.

If blockchains are a new way to implement trusted transactions without trusted intermediaries, soon we'll end up with intermediary-less trust. Policy makers who regulated "trusted" institutions like banks will face a dilemma. How can you regulate something that is evaporating? They will need to update their old regulations.

Intermediary-controlled trust came with some friction, but now, with the blockchain, we can have frictionless trust. So, when trust is "free" (even if it still needs to be earned), what happens next? Naturally, trust will follow the path of least resistance, and will become gradually decentralized towards the edges of the network.

Blockchains also enable assets and value to be exchanged, providing a new, speedy rail for moving value of all kinds without unnecessary intermediaries.

As back-end infrastructure, blockchains are metaphorically the ultimate, non-stop computers. Once launched, they never go down, because of the incredible amount of resiliency they offer. There is no single point of failure unlike how bank systems have gone down, cloud-based services have gone down, but bona fide blockchains keep computing.

The Internet was about replacing some intermediaries. Now the blockchain is about replacing other intermediaries once again. But it's also about creating new ones. And so was the Web. Current intermediaries will need to figure out how their roles will be affected, while others are angling to take a piece of the new pie in the race to "decentralize everything."

The world is preoccupied with dissecting, analyzing and prognosticating on the blockchain's future; technologists, entrepreneurs, and enterprises are wondering if it is to be considered vitamin or poison.

Today, we're saying blockchain does this or that, but tomorrow blockchains will be rather invisible; we will talk more about what they enable. Just like the Internet or the Web, and just like databases, the blockchain brings with it a new language.

From the mid-1950s forward, as IT evolved, we became accustomed to a new language: mainframes, databases, networks, servers, software, operating systems, and programming languages. Since the early 1990s, the Internet ushered in another lexicon: browsing, website, Java, blogging, TCP/IP, SMTP, HTTP, URLs, and HTML. Today, the blockchain brings with it yet another new repertoire: consensus algorithms, smart contracts, distributed ledgers, oracles, digital wallets, and transaction blocks.

Block by block, we will accumulate our own chains of knowledge, and we will learn and understand the blockchain, what it changes, and the implications of such change.

Today, we google for everything, mostly information or products.

Tomorrow, we will perform the equivalent of "googling" to verify records, identities, authenticity, rights, work done, titles, contracts, and other valuable asset-related processes. There will be digital ownership certificates for everything. Just like we cannot double spend digital money anymore (thanks to Satoshi Nakamoto's invention), we will not be able to double copy or forge official certificates once they are certified on a blockchain. That was a missing piece of the information revolution, which the blockchain fixes.

I still remember the initial excitement around being able to track a shipped package on the Web when FedEx introduced this capability for the first time in 1994. Today, we take that type of service for granted, but this particular feature was a watershed use case that demonstrated what we could do on the early Web. The underlying message was that a previously enclosed private service could become openly accessible by anyone with Internet access. A whole host of services followed: online banking, filing taxes, buying products, trading stocks, checking on orders, and many others. Just as we access services that search public databases, we will search a new class of services that will check blockchains to confirm the veracity of information. Information access will not be enough. We will also want to ask for truth access, and we will ask if modifications were made to particular records, expecting the utmost transparency from those who hold them. The blockchain promises to serve up and expose transparency in its rawest forms.

The old adage "Is it in the database?" will be replaced by "Is it on the blockchain?"

Is the blockchain more complicated than the Web? Most definitely.

Allow me to take you on this journey to decipher it.

THE BUSINESS BLOCKCHAIN

□-□-①-□-□

WHAT IS THE BLOCKCHAIN?

"If you cannot understand it without an explanation, you cannot understand it with an explanation."

—HARUKI MURAKAMI

PAY CLOSE ATTENTION. This chapter is probably the most important in the book, because it attempts to offer a foundational explanation of the blockchain. It is the first stage of this book's promise to give you a holistic view of the blockchain's potential.

Understanding blockchains is tricky. You need to understand their message before you can appreciate their potential. In addition to their technological capabilities, blockchains carry with them philosophical, cultural, and ideological underpinnings that must also be understood.

Unless you're a software developer, blockchains are not a product that you just turn on, and use. Blockchains will enable other products that you will use, while you may not know there is a blockchain behind them, just as you do not know the complexities behind what you are currently accessing on the Web.

Once you start to imagine the blockchains' possibilities on your own, without continuously thinking about trying to understand them at the same time, you will be in a different stage of your maturity for exploiting them.

It is my belief that the knowledge transfer behind understanding the blockchain is easier than the knowledge about knowing where they will fit. It's like learning how to drive a car. I could teach you how to drive one, but cannot predict where you will take it. Only you know your particular business or situation, and only you will be able to figure out where blockchains fit, after you have learned what they can do. Of course, we will first go together on road tests and racing tracks to give you some ideas.

VISITING SATOSHI'S PAPER

When Tim Berners-Lee created the first World Wide Web page in 1990, he wrote: "When we link information in the Web, we enable ourselves to discover facts, create ideas, buy and sell things, and forge new relationships at a speed and scale that was unimaginable in the analogue era."

In that short statement, Berners-Lee predicted search, publishing, e-commerce, e-mail, and social media, all at once, by a single stroke. The Bitcoin equivalent to that type of prescience by someone who just created something spectacular can be found in Satoshi Nakamato's 2008 paper, "Bitcoin: A Peer-to-Peer Electronic Cash System,"[1] arguably the root of modern blockchain-based cryptocurrency innovation.

The paper's abstract depicts Bitcoin's foundation, and it explains its first principles:

- A purely *peer-to-peer* version of electronic cash would allow online payments to be sent *directly from one party to another without going through a financial institution.*

- A *trusted third party is not required* to prevent double-spending.

- We propose a *solution* to the double-spending problem *using a peer-to-peer network.*

- *The network timestamps transactions* by hashing them into an ongoing chain of hash-based proof-of-work, forming *a record that cannot be changed without redoing the proof-of-work.*

- The longest chain not only serves as proof of the sequence of events witnessed, but proof that it came from the largest pool of CPU power. As long as *a majority of CPU power is controlled by nodes that are not cooperating to attack the network,* they'll generate the longest chain and outpace attackers.

- The network itself requires minimal structure. Messages are broadcast on a best-effort basis, and *nodes can leave and rejoin the network at will, accepting the longest proof-of-work chain as proof of what happened while they were gone.*

If you are a non-technical reader, and you focus on the italicized parts, you will start to get the gist of it. Please re-read the above points, until you have internalized Nakamoto's sequential logic! Seriously. You will need to believe and accept that validating peer-to-peer transactions is entirely possible by just letting the network perform a trust duty, without central interference or hand-holding.

Paraphrasing Nakamoto's paper, we should be left with these points:

- Peer-to-peer electronic transactions and interactions
- Without financial institutions
- Cryptographic proof instead of central trust
- Put trust in the network instead of in a central institution

As it turns out, the "blockchain" is that technology invention behind Bitcoin, and what makes this possible. With Satoshi's abstract still in your mind, let us dive deeper with three different but complementary definitions of the blockchain: a technical, business, and legal one.

Technically, the blockchain is a back-end database that maintains a distributed ledger that can be inspected openly.

Business-wise, the blockchain is an exchange network for moving transactions, value, assets between peers, without the assistance of intermediaries.

Legally speaking, the blockchain validates transactions, replacing previously trusted entities.

TECHNICAL   Back-end database that maintains a distributed ledger, openly.

BUSINESS   Exchange network for moving value between peers.

LEGAL   A transaction validation mechanism, not requiring intermediary assistance.

Blockchain Capabilities = Technical + Business + Legal.

THE WEB, ALL OVER AGAIN

The past is not an accurate compass to the future, but understanding where we came from helps us gain an enlightened perspective and a better context for where we are going. The blockchain is simply part of the continuation of the history of Internet technology, represented by the Web, as it carries on its journey to infiltrate our world, businesses, society, and government, and across the several cycles and phases that often become visible only in the rearview mirror.

Whereas the Internet was first rolled out in 1983, it was the World Wide Web that gave us its watershed evolutionary moment, because it made information and information-based services openly and instantly available to anyone on earth who had access to the Web.

In the same way that billions of people around the world are currently connected to the Web, millions, and then billions of people, will be connected to blockchains. We should not be surprised if the velocity of blockchain usage propagation surpasses the historical Web users growth.

By mid-2016, 47% of the world's 7.4 billion population had an Internet connection. In 1995, that number was less than 1%. It took until 2005 to reach one billion Web users. In contrast, cellular phone usage galloped faster, passing the number of landlines in 2002, and surpassing the world's population in 2013. As for websites, in 2016, their total number hovered at around one billion. Quite possibly, blockchains will grow into several flavors, and will become as easily configurable as launching a website on Wordpress or Squarespace.

The blockchain's usage growth has an advantage on the Web's trajectory, because its starting point is amplified along four segments: Web users, cellular phone users, website owners, and any "thing" that gains benefits from being connected, and becoming a "smart thing." This means that blockchain usage will ride on these four categories, instead of purely seeking new users.

ONE OR SEVERAL BLOCKCHAINS?

There are no previous paradigms for the blockchain. It is not a new version of TCP/IP, the Internet network protocol. It is not another whole Internet either. In 2015, some proponents of a single Bitcoin blockchain lamented the existence of several blockchains. The blockchain was seen via a one-dimensional lens (Bitcoin maximalism[2]), by taking a similar view as the Internet. Yes, it's good there is only one Internet, as it would have never propagated as it did. But the blockchain is a different construct. It is more of a new protocol that sits on top of the Internet, just as the World Wide Web sits on top of the Internet via its own technology standards.

The blockchain is part database, part development platform, part network enabler, so we need many instances of it and variations thereof. As an overlay on top of the Internet, blockchains can take many forms of implementations. Blockchains can be seen as a trust layer, an exchange medium, a secure pipe, a set of decentralized capabilities, and even more.

That said, there are many analogies between the Web's early years and today's blockchain's evolution, in terms of how the technology will be adopted.

Let us not forget that it took about three years for most companies to fully understand the Web's potential (1994–1997 roughly), after its initial commercialization, and it took seven years after the Internet's 1983 launch for the Web to come into play. There is no doubt the blockchain will remain a semi-mysterious, semi-complex phenomena for the period 2015–2018, just as it took Bitcoin three quiet years (2009–2012) before it became more visibly known to the general public.

INTRODUCTION TO BLOCKCHAIN APPLICATIONS

The Web could not exist without the Internet. And blockchains could not be without the Internet. The Web made the Internet more useful, because people were more interested in using the information, than figuring out how to hook up computers together. Blockchain applications need the Internet, but they can bypass the Web, and give us another version that is more decentralized, and perhaps more equitable. That is one of the biggest promises of blockchain technology.

BLOCKCHAINS, LIKE THE WEB, NEED THE INTERNET

There is more than one way to build blockchain applications. You can build them natively on a blockchain, or you could mix them in an existing Web application, and we will call that flavor, "hybrid blockchain applications."

FLAVORS OF BLOCKCHAIN APPLICATIONS

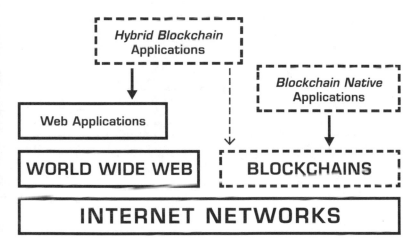

Since the Internet is comprised of a public version and several private variations, blockchains will also follow that path. Therefore, we will have public and private blockchains. Some will be natively bolted to a blockchain, whereas others might be a hybrid implementation that is part of an existing Web or private application.

FOUR TYPES OF BLOCKCHAIN APPLICATIONS

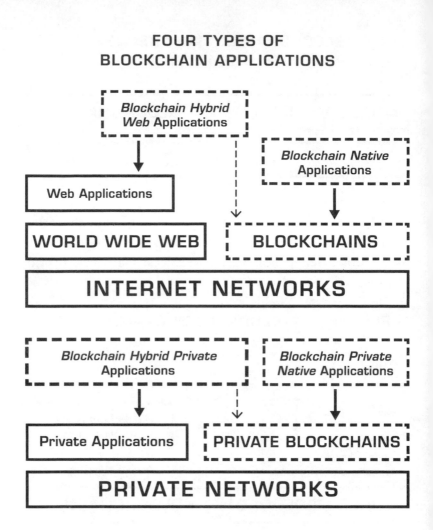

THE BLOCKCHAIN'S NARRATIVE IS STRONG

A sign of strong impact for a technology or trend is whether it has a strong narrative. What's the difference between a story and a narrative? Whereas a story is usually consistent and known, a narrative creates more individual stories for whomever interacts with that trend.

John Hagel explained that difference well:[3]

Stories are self-contained—they have a beginning, a middle and an end. Narratives on the other hand are open-ended—the outcome is unresolved, yet to be determined. Second, stories are about me, the storyteller, or other people; they are not about you. In contrast, the resolution of narratives depends on the choice you make and the actions you take—you will determine the outcome.

The Internet had a strong narrative. If you ask various people how they use the Internet, or what it means to them, you would undoubtedly hear different answers, because each person takes the Internet and makes it their own, depending on their own adaptation of its usages.

The blockchain has a strong narrative because it sparks our imagination.

According to Hagel, these are specific benefits that narratives provide:

DIFFERENTIATION – it helps you to stand out from the crowd

LEVERAGE – it mobilizes people outside your company

DISTRIBUTED INNOVATION – it spurs innovation in unexpected directions

ATTRACTION – it draws people by the opportunity and the challenge you have laid out

RELATIONSHIPS – it spurs sustained relationships with others that have fallen under the spell of your narrative

John Hagel goes on specifying that "it's about connecting with and mobilizing others beyond the boundaries of ...." Replace the dots by "blockchain," and you will get a powerful foundation for a strong and long lasting blockchain narrative.

A META TECHNOLOGY

The blockchain is a meta technology because it affects other technologies, and it is made up of several technologies itself. It is as an overlay of computers and networks that are built on top of the Internet. When you examine the architectural layers of a blockchain, you will find it is comprised of several pieces: a database, a software application, a number of computers connected to each other, clients to access it, a software environment to develop on it, tools to monitor it, and other pieces (that will be covered in Chapter 6).

Blockchain is not just any new technology. It is a type of technology that challenges other existing software technologies, because it has the potential to replace or supplement existing practices. In essence, it is technology that changes other technology.

The last time we witnessed such a catalytic technology dates back to the Web's arrival. The Web also changed how we wrote software applications, and it brought along with it new software technology that challenged and replaced previous ones. In 1993, HTML, a markup language changed publishing. In 1995, Java, a Web programming language changed programming. A few years earlier, TCP/IP, a computer network protocol had started to change networking by making it fully interoperable, globally.

From a software development point of view, one of the biggest paradigm shifts that the blockchain claims is in challenging the function and monopoly of the traditional database as we currently know it. Therefore we need to deeply understand how the blockchain makes us rethink the existing database constructs.

The blockchain is changing how we write applications via a new form of scripting languages that can program business logic as smart contracts that are enforced on the blockchain.

SOFTWARE, GAME THEORY AND CRYPTOGRAPHY

Another way to understand the blockchain is in seeing it as a triad of combustion of the known fields of 1) game theory, 2) cryptography science, and 3) software engineering. Separately, these fields have existed for a long time, but for the first time, they have together intersected harmoniously and morphed inside blockchain technology.

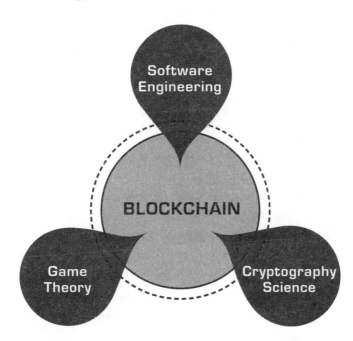

Game theory is 'the study of mathematical models of conflict and cooperation between intelligent rational decision-makers.'[4] And this is related to the blockchain because the Bitcoin blockchain, originally conceived by Satoshi Nakamoto, had to solve a known game theory conundrum called the Byzantine Generals Problem.[5] Solving that problem consists in mitigating any attempts by a small number of unethical Generals who would otherwise become traitors, and lie about coordinating their attack to guarantee victory.

This is accomplished by enforcing a process for verifying the work that was put into crafting these messages, and time-limiting the requirement for seeing untampered messages in order to ensure their validity. Implementing a "Byzantine Fault Tolerance" is important because it starts with the assumption that you cannot trust anyone, and yet it delivers assurance that the transaction has traveled and arrived safely based on trusting the network during its journey, while surviving potential attacks.

There are fundamental implications for this new method of reaching safety in the finality of a transaction, because it questions the existence and roles of current trusted intermediaries, who held the traditional authority on validating transactions. This makes us ponder the existential question: why do we need a central authority to ensure central trust, if we can accomplish the same trustworthiness when the transaction travels from one peer to another, via a network where trust is embedded in it?

Cryptography science is used in multiple places to provide security for a blockchain network, and it rests on three basic concepts: hashing, keys, and digital signatures. A "hash" is a unique fingerprint that helps to verify that a certain piece of information has not been altered, without the need to actually see it. Keys are used in at least a combination of two: a public and a private one. For analogy, imagine a door that needs two keys to open it. In this case, the public key is used by the sender to encrypt information that can only be decrypted by the owner of the private key. You never reveal your private key. A digital signature is a mathematical computation that is used to prove the authenticity of a (digital) message or document.

Cryptography is based on the public/private hegemony, which is the yin-yang of the blockchain: public visibility, but private inspection. It's a bit like your home address. You can publish your home address publicly, but that does not give any information about what your home looks like on the inside. You'll need your private key to enter your private home, and since you have claimed that address as yours, no one else can claim a similar address as being theirs.

Although the concepts of cryptography have been around for a while, software engineers are feasting on combining it with game theory innovation, to produce the overall constructs of blockchains, where seeming uncertainty is mitigated with overwhelming mathematical certainty.

THE DATABASE VS. THE LEDGER

We have transactions that can get validated without a third party. Now, you're thinking—how about databases? We have always thought that databases are trusted repositories for holding assets.

In the case of the blockchain, the ledger is that irrefutable record that holds the register of transactions that have been validated by the blockchain network.

Let us illustrate the impact of this situation: the database versus the (blockchain) ledger.

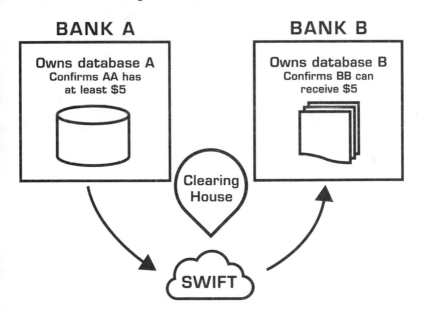

When you open a bank account, you have really abdicated authority to your bank on that "account." In reality, they provided you the illusion of access and activity visibility on it. Every time you want to move money, pay someone or deposit money, the bank is giving you explicit access because you gave them implicit trust over your affairs. But that "access" is also another illusion. It is really an access to a database record that says you have such amount of money. Again, they fooled you by giving you the illusion that you "own" that money. But they hold the higher authority because they own the database that points to that entry that says that you have the money, and you assume that you have your money.

Banking is complex, but I tried to simplify the above illustration to emphasize the fact that a given bank owns the control hierarchy for granting or denying access to money they hold. The same concept applies for any digital assets (stocks, bonds, securities) that a financial institution might hold on your behalf.

Enter the blockchain.

In its most basic form, that same scenario can happen without the complexities depicted above. A user can send money to another, via a special wallet, and the blockchain network does the authentication, validation and transfer, typically within 10 minutes, with or without a cryptocurrency exchange in the middle.

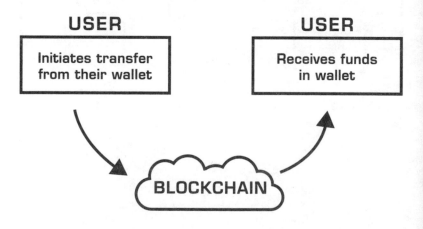

USER

Initiates transfer from their wallet

USER

Receives funds in wallet

BLOCKCHAIN

That is the magic of the blockchain in its simplest form. That is why I suggest to anyone who is going to get involved in implementing the blockchain to experience performing this type of transaction with their own wallet, by either downloading one of the many available versions, or by signing-up to a local Bitcoin exchange that exists wherever you live. Once you do, you will realize the true meaning of "no intermediaries," and you will start to question why we still need the current intermediaries.

LOOKING BACK SO WE CAN LOOK FORWARD

So, where does the blockchain fit in the overall context of the various eras of technology evolution?

In 2003, Nicholas G. Carr dropped a seminal article[6] in the *Harvard Business Review*, "IT Does not Matter," that shook the Information Technologies corporate circles and questioned their strategic relevance. He wrote:

> *What makes a resource truly strategic—what gives it the capacity to be the basis for a sustained competitive advantage—is not ubiquity but scarcity. You only gain an edge over rivals by having or doing something that they cannot have or do. By now, the core functions of IT—data storage, data processing, and data transport—have become available and affordable to all.*

Although Carr was vigorously debated for another two years following that article, the writing was already on the wall, coinciding with the advent of the Web as a powerful new computing platform. The Web caught CIOs by surprise, and put most of them in disarray for at least three years, especially that many of them were more focused on the year 2000 date compliance issue. In reality, IT's decline had started when the Web arrived, because the Web provided some competitive advantages to those who mastered it early.

As depicted in this chart, the end of IT supremacy was followed by the Internet years, which in turn will be followed by the Blockchain's promise.

DEFINING TECHNOLOGY ERAS

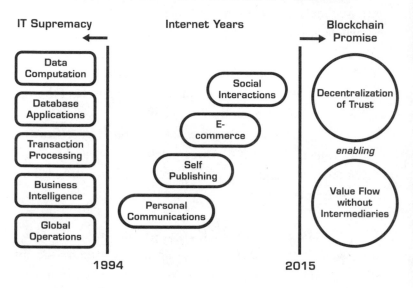

Another way to see continuity in technology's evolution is by depicting the various phases of the Web's evolution, and seeing that the blockchain is yet another new phase, focused on peer-to-peer, trust-based asset transactions. Let us remember the key mini-revolutions that the Internet brought us since 1994: Personal Communications, Self-Publishing, E-Commerce, and the Social Web. In hindsight, each of these four phases was defined by the functions they disrupted: the post-office, print media, supply chains/physical stores, and the real world.

PHASE	GOAL	DISRUPTING	OUTCOME
Communications	Reach anyone in the world	Post office	Personal Communications
Publishing	Spread ideas	Print media	Self-publishing
Commerce	Trade	Supply chains and physical stores	E-Commerce
Social Interactions	Connect with friends	Real world	Social Web
Asset Transactions	Manage what you own	Existing custodians	Trust-based Services

The irony of this situation is that blockchain-based applications can replace any Web application. Although we think the Web brought us information publishing, communications and e-commerce, those very functions will be threatened by new versions that rest on peer-to-peer protocols that are anchored by blockchain technologies.

UNPACKING THE BLOCKCHAIN

Let us continue revealing the many layers of the blockchain! If there is one main point that I will keep drilling upon, it is to emphasize that the blockchain is not one item, thing, trend, or feature. It is many pieces all at once, some of them working together, and others independently.

When the Internet started to get commercialized around 1995, we often described it as multi-purpose kind of phenomenon. In my previous book, *Opening Digital Markets*, in 1997, I described the Internet as having "five multiple identities," and added that "each one must be taken advantage of by developing a different strategy." The Web was simultaneously a Network, a Development Platform, a Transaction Platform, a Medium, and a Marketplace. (We didn't see the Community / Social Network aspect then, as it surfaced later.)

The blockchain takes that multiplicity of functions further. It exhibits simultaneously the following ten properties:

1. Cryptocurrency
2. Computing Infrastructure
3. Transaction Platform
4. Decentralized Database
5. Distributed Accounting Ledger
6. Development Platform
7. Open Source Software
8. Financial Services Marketplace
9. Peer-to-Peer Network
10. Trust Services Layer

Let us dive into each one of them, as the first step in establishing a foundational understanding of the blockchain.

1. Digital Cryptocurrency

The digital currency function is probably the most "visible" element in a blockchain, especially if the blockchain is a public one, for example, Bitcoin (BTC) or Ethereum (ETH). Cryptocurrency is generally an economic proxy to the viable operations and security of a blockchain. Sometimes it is represented by a token, which is another form of related representation of an underlying cryptocurrency.

One of the challenging issues with cryptocurrencies is their price volatility, which is enough to keep most consumers away. In a 2014 paper describing a method for stabilizing cryptocurrency, Robert Sams quoted Nick Szabo: "The main volatility in bitcoin comes from variability in speculation, which in turn is due to the genuine uncertainty about its future. More efficient liquidity mechanisms do not help reduce genuine uncertainty." As cryptocurrency gains more acceptance and understanding, its future will be less uncertain, resulting in a more stable and gradual adoption curve.

Cryptocurrency can have a "production" role for compensating miners who win rewards when they successfully validate transactions. Cryptocurrency can also have a "consumption" role when paying a small fee for running a smart contract (e.g., Ethereum's ETH), or as a transaction fee equivalent (e.g., Ripple's XRP or Bitcoin's BTC). These economic incentives and costs are put in place to prevent abuse of the blockchain. In a more advanced usage case, the token can be used as a unit of internal value, for example in Distributed Autonomous Organizations (DAOs), a subject that will be covered later in Chapters 5 and 7 of this book.

Outside of the blockchain's operations proper, cryptocurrency is just like any other currency. It can be traded on exchanges, and it can be used to buy or sell goods and services. Cryptocurrency is very efficient inside blockchain networks, but there is friction every time it crosses into the real world of traditional currency (also called "fiat currency").

2. Decentralized Computing Infrastructure

The blockchain can also be seen as a software design approach that binds a number of computers together that commonly obey the same "consensus" process for releasing or recording what information they hold, and where all related interactions are verified by cryptography.

From a physical perspective, networked computer servers are what really powers blockchains. But developers do not need to set up these servers, and that is part of the magic of a blockchain. As contrasted with the Web where an HTTP (Hypertext Transfer Protocol) request is sent to the server, with blockchain apps, the network makes a request to the blockchain.

3. Transaction Platform

A blockchain network can validate a variety of value-related transactions relating to digital money or assets that have been digitized.

Every time a consensus is reached, a transaction is recorded on a "block" which is a storage space. The blockchain keeps track of these transactions that can be later verified as having taken place. The blockchain is therefore this giant transaction processing platform, capable of handling microtransactions and large value transactions alike.

If we are to equate blockchains to other transactions processing networks, what comes to mind is their processing throughput, which is measured in transactions per second (TPS). As a reference, in 2015, VISA handled an average of 2,000 TPS on their VisaNet, with a peak rate of 4,000 TPS, and a peak capacity of 56,000 TPS. During 2015, PayPal processed a total 4.9 billion payments,[7] equivalent to 155 TPS. As of 2016, the Bitcoin blockchain was far from these numbers, hovering at 5–7 TPS, but with prospects of largely exceeding it due to advances in sidechain technology and expected increases in the Bitcoin block size. Some other blockchains are faster than Bitcoin's. For example, Ethereum started with 10 TPS in 2015, edging towards 50–100 TPS in 2017, and targeting 50,000–100,000 TPS by 2019.[8] Private blockchains are even faster because they have less security requirements, and we are seeing 1,000–10,000 TPS in 2016, going up to 2,000–15,000 TPS in 2017, and potentially an unlimited ceiling beyond 2019. Finally, linking blockchain's output to clustered database technology might push these transactional throughput limits even higher, leading to a positive development.

4. Decentralized Database

The blockchain shatters the database/transaction processing paradigm. In 2014, I made the strong assertion that the blockchain is the new database, and warned developers to get ready to rewrite everything.

A blockchain is like a place where you store any data semi-publicly in a linear container space (the block). Anyone can verify that you've placed that information, because the container has your signature on it, but only you (or a program) can unlock what's inside the container, because only you hold the private keys to that data, securely.

So the blockchain behaves almost like a database, except that part of the information stored, its "header," is public. Admittedly, blockchains are not very efficient databases, but that's OK. Their job is not to replace large databases, but rather, it is the job of software developers to figure out how they can re-write their applications to take advantage of the blockchain's state transitions capabilities.

5. Shared, Distributed Accounting Ledger

The blockchain is also a distributed, public, time-stamped asset ledger that keeps track of every transaction ever processed on its network, allowing a user's computer to verify the validity of each transaction such that there can never be any double-counting. This ledger can be shared across multiple parties, and it can be private, public, or semi-private.

Although being a distributed ledger of transactions is a popular way to describe blockchains, and some see it as the killer app, it is only one of its characteristics.

6. Software Development Platform

For developers, a blockchain is first and foremost a set of software technologies. Yes, they have an underlying political and socie tal underpinning (decentralization), but they bring with them technological novelties. This new set of development tools is an exciting event for software engineers. The blockchain includes technologies for building a new breed of applications, ones that are decentralized and cryptographically secure.

Also, blockchains can have a variety of APIs, including a transaction scripting language, a P2P nodes communications API, and a client API to check transactions on the network. I will cover the software development aspect in more details in Chapter 6 of this book.

7. Open Source Software

Most robust blockchains are open sourced, which not only means that the source of the software is public, it also means that innovation can happen in a collaborative way, on top of the core software.

For example, the core Bitcoin protocol is open source. Since its initial development by its creator Satoshi Nakamoto, it has been maintained by a group of "core developers," who continue to enhance it over time. In addition, thousands of independent developers innovate with complementary products, services, and applications that take advantage of the Bitcoin protocol robustness.

The fact that blockchain software is open source is a powerful feature. The more open the core of a blockchain is, the stronger the ecosystem around it will become.

8. Financial Services Marketplace

Money is at the heart of cryptocurrency-based blockchains. When cryptocurrency is treated like any currency, it can become part of a financial instrument, leading to the development of a variety of new financial products.

Blockchains offer an incredible innovation environment for the next generation of financial services. As cryptocurrency volatilities subside, these will become popular. Derivatives, options, swaps, synthetic instruments, investments, loans, and many other traditional instruments will have their cryptocurrency version, therefore creating a new financial services trading marketplace.

9. Peer-to-Peer Network

There is nothing "central" about blockchains. Architecturally, the base layer of the blockchain is a peer-to-peer network. A blockchain pushes for decentralization via peer processing at its node locations. The network is really the computer. You verify each other transaction at the peer-to-peer level. In essence, a blockchain could be regarded as a thin computing cloud that is truly decentralized.

Any user can reach and transact with another user instantly, no matter where they are in the universe, and regardless of business hours. No intermediary is needed to filter, block, or delay a transaction between any two or more users, or between nodes that are consuming a transaction. Any node on the network is allowed to offer services based on their knowledge of transactions everywhere else in that network.

In addition to creating a technical P2P network, blockchains also create a marketplace of users. Blockchain networks and applications on top of them create their own (distributed) economies, with a variety of sizes and vibrancy. So, blockchains bring with them an economic model, and that is a key feature that will be expanded upon later in this book.

10. Trust Services Layer

All blockchains commonly hold trust as an atomic unit of service. In essence, it is a function and a service that is delivered. But trust does not apply only to transactions. It is extended to data, services, processes, identity, business logic, terms of an agreement, or physical objects. It applies to almost anything that can be digitized as a (smart) asset with an inherent or related value attached to it.

Now, imagine the possible mashup of innovations that will spring out on top of these 10 powerful features and characteristics. By combining them together, you'll start to imagine the incredible enabling powers of blockchains.

STATE TRANSITIONS AND STATE MACHINES— WHAT ARE THEY?

The blockchain is not for everything. And not everything fits the blockchain paradigm. The blockchain is a "state machine," which is another concept that needs to be understood.

In technical terms, a state just means "stored information" at a specific point in time. A state machine is a computer or device that remembers the status of something at a given instant in time. Based on some inputs, that status might change, and it provides a resulting output for these implemented changes. Keeping track of transitions of these states is important and that's what the blockchain does well, and in a way that is immutable. In contrast, a database's record is mutable, because it can be re-written many times over. Not all databases have audit trails, and even if they do, an audit trail could be destroyed or lost, because it is not tamper proof. In the blockchain, the transition history is a persistent part of the information about that state. In the Ethereum blockchain, a distinct "state tree" is stored, representing the current balance of each address, and a "transaction list" representing the transactions between the current block and previous blocks in each block.

State machines are a good fit for implementing distributed systems that have to be fault-tolerant.

THE CONSENSUS ALGORITHMS

At the heart of understanding the severity of the blockchain paradigm shift lies the basic understanding of the concept of "decentralized consensus," a key tenet of the cryptography-based computing revolution.

Decentralized consensus breaks the old paradigm of centralized consensus, that is, when one central database used to rule transaction validity. A decentralized scheme (which blockchain protocols are based on), transfers authority and trust to a decentralized virtual network, and enables its nodes to continuously and sequentially record transactions on a public "block," creating a unique "chain," the blockchain. Each successive block contains a "hash" (a unique fingerprint) of the previous code, therefore cryptography (via hash codes) is used to secure the authentication of the transaction source and removes the need for a central intermediary. The combination of cryptography and blockchain technology ensures there is never a duplicate recording of the same transaction. What's important here is that with this degree of unbundling, the consensus logic is separate from the application itself, therefore applications can be written to be organically decentralized, and that is the spark for a variety of system-changing innovations in the software architecture of applications, whether they are money or non-money related.

You could think of consensus as the first layer of a decentralized architecture. It is the basis for the underlying protocol governing a blockchain's operation.

A consensus algorithm is the nucleus of a blockchain representing the method or protocol that commits the transaction. It is important, because we need to trust these transactions. As a business user, you do not need to understand the exact ways that these algorithms work, as long as you believe in their security and reliability.

Bitcoin initiated the Proof-of-Work (POW) consensus method, and it can be regarded as the granddaddy of these algorithms. POW rests on the popular Practical Byzantine Fault Tolerant[9] algorithm that allows transactions to be safely committed according to a given state. An alternative to POW for achieving consensus is Proof-of-Stake.[10] There are other consensus protocols such as RAFT, DPOS, and Paxos, but we are not going into that slippery slope of comparing them to each other, because they will be seen as standard plumbing over time. What will matter more is the robustness of the tools and middleware technologies that are being built on top of the algorithms, as well as the ecosystem of value-added players that surround them.

One of the drawbacks of the Proof-of-Work algorithm is that it is not environmentally friendly, because it requires large amounts of processing power from specialized machines that generate excessive energy. A strong contender to POW will be the Proof-of-Stake (POS) algorithm which relies on the concept of virtual mining and token-based voting, a process that does not require the intensity of computer processing as the POW, and one that promises to reach security in a more cost-effective manner.

Finally, when discussing consensus algorithm, you need to consider the "permissioning" method, which determines who gets to control and participate in the consensus process. The three popular choices for the type of permissioning are:

1. Public (e.g., POW, POS, Delegated POS)
2. Private (uses secret keys to establish authority within a confined blockchain)
3. Semi-private (e.g., consortium-based, uses traditional Byzantine Fault Tolerance in a federated manner)

KEY IDEAS FROM CHAPTER ONE

1. The blockchain is a layer of technology on top of the Internet, just like the World Wide Web.

2. A blockchain has technical, business and legal definitions.

3. Cryptographic proof is the trusted method that blockchains utilize to confirm the validity and finality of transactions between parties.

4. The blockchain will redefine the role of existing intermediaries (if they accept to change), while creating new intermediaries, therefore it will disrupt the traditional boundaries of value.

5. The blockchain has ten characteristics, and they all need to be understood in a holistic manner.

NOTES

1. Bitcoin: A Peer-to-Peer Electronic Cash System, https://bitcoin.org/en/bitcoin-paper.

2. Bitcoin "maximalism" refers to the opinion that solely supports Bitcoin at the expense of all other blockchain or cryptocurrency related projects, because maximalists believe we only a need a single blockchain, and single currency in order to achieve desired network effects benefits.

3. The Untapped Potential of Corporate Narratives. http://edgeperspectives.typepad.com/edge_perspectives/2013/10/the-untapped-potential-of-corporate-narratives.html.

4. Myerson, Roger B. (1991). *Game Theory: Analysis of Conflict*, Harvard University Press.

5. Leslie Lamport, Robert Shostak, and Marshall Pease, *The Byzantine Generals Problem*. http://research.microsoft.com/en-us/um/people/lamport/pubs/byz.pdf.

6. *IT Does not Matter*, https://hbr.org/2003/05/it-doesnt-matter.

7. PayPal website, https://www.paypal.com/webapps/mpp/about.

8. Personal communication with Vitalik Buterin, February 2016.

9. Byzantine fault tolerance, https://en.wikipedia.org/wiki/Byzantine_fault_tolerance.

10. Proof-of-stake, https://en.wikipedia.org/wiki/Proof-of-stake.

□-□-2-□-□

HOW BLOCKCHAIN TRUST
INFILTRATES

*"I cannot understand why people are frightened
of new ideas. I'm frightened of the old ones."*

—JOHN CAGE

REACHING CONSENSUS is at the heart of a blockchain's operations. But the blockchain does it in a decentralized way that breaks the old paradigm of centralized consensus, when one central database used to rule transaction validity. A decentralized scheme (which the blockchain is based on) transfers authority and trust to a decentralized network and enables its nodes to continuously and sequentially record their transactions on a public "block," creating a unique "chain"—the blockchain.

Of course, the blockchain is destined to affect almost everything. But the challenge is in knowing how, when, and what the impact will be. The first chapter was essential for laying out the multiple capabilities of the blockchain technology, paving the way for your understanding of its usage, and making you believe that peer-to-peer transactions *can* be finalized on the blockchain, without known intermediaries, except for the blockchain itself.

Blockchain is not a one-trick pony. It is a multi-headed beast that takes many forms.

If you see it as a technology, then you will implement it as a technology. If you see it as a business change enabler, then you will think about business processes. If you discern the legal implications, you will be emboldened by its new governance characteristics. And if you see it as a blank sheet of paper for designing new possibilities that either didn't exist before, or that challenge existing legacies, then you will want to get very creative at dreaming up these new opportunities.

At its genesis, blockchain (and certainly Bitcoin) is a technology that came to life to challenge the status quo, without preconceived sympathy to what the status quo held on to. Nowhere in the Nakamoto paper was there a mention about integrating with the existing world. Much of that came as an afterthought by those who later interpreted and applied Bitcoin in so many different ways.

At the macro level, the future of blockchain technology will unfold in ways that may not be so different from how the Web unfolded, from a market deployment and acceptance perspective.

A NEW TRUST LAYER

The blockchain disrupts and redefines our commonly accepted beliefs around trust.

If we exclude spiritual, philosophical, and emotional connotations when we think of trust, in the business transactional sense, we think of the following meanings: *reliance, predictability, confidence, truth, assurance, credence, certainty, certitude, responsibility, and dependence.*

As citizens or business people, let us pick on a few commonly trusted institutions we interact with on a daily basis: banks, governments, credit card companies, and utilities companies.

We typically trust these organizations because most of them do a good job most of the time, and they deliver, armed with our trust.

Banks do not steal our money, and they let us withdraw it anytime we would like. Governments deliver services in return for taxes they collect. Credit card companies let us borrow money, with the added convenience of ubiquitous usage. And utilities companies deliver electricity, water, or telecommunications services, as long as we keep paying our bills.

Nothing wrong with that picture, you might think. Yet, for each of these organizations, we also can think of cases where the trust that we seemingly granted them also could be eroded, abused, neglected, forgotten, or sometimes become too expensive.

Banks will delay clearing our checks, even if they can immediately debit our accounts when we buy something. Governments easily squander our tax money, but we cannot see that, or readily prove it. Credit card companies charge us 23% in interest, even when the prime rate is only at 1%. Utility companies subject us to service outages or degradations without compensating us; or worse, they can change their rates or terms with little notice.

There is a cause and effect relationship at play. These institutions can get away with these extreme cases (the unfortunate effects), because we trust them otherwise 95% of the time, and we are tolerant towards their trust failures. So what does the blockchain have to do with this?

The blockchain will not do much to save us the 5% of the time when the above "bad" cases happened. But, we will argue that the blockchain can do a lot in improving transparency for the remaining 95% of the time when transactions are trusted, so that the unfortunate effects of trust failures could be eliminated (or at least dampened). By giving us more transparency about their trust layers, organizations would fail less, not just because they will be more on guard, or fear getting questioned, but because they can decentralize their potential failures, and allow us to be part of early warning systems, and consequently, that should result in lowering their overall risks.

The blockchain offers a degree of transparency and access to truth that can prevent breaches of trust. What if this new technology could redefine the trust function that intermediaries used to perform, and deliver a similar outcome, with added benefits? Blockchains offer truth and transparency as a base layer. But most trusted institutions do not offer transparency or truth. It will be an interesting encounter.

DECENTRALIZATION OF TRUST—WHAT DOES IT MEAN?

With the blockchain, the trust train is moving to a new destination. It is shifting from humans and central organizations to computers and decentralized organizations, via an underlying blockchain-based decentralized consensus protocol that governs its delivery.

The previous paradigm was to channel our attention towards trusted authorities, and allow them to handle our transactions, our data, our legal status, our possessions, and our wealth.

In a new paradigm, some parts of central trust processes will be relegated to blockchains that can serve that trust function. If traditional "trust checking" has become a costly, friction-rich element of a given process or service, maybe the blockchain could offer a solution.

The central question is: can the blockchain give us Trust 2.0, a better form of trust that does not always depend on central intermediaries who may have become too big to fail, too bureaucratic to see risk, or too slow to change?

Here are seven principles that we will need to believe in, if we are to believe in the future of decentralized trust:

1. It would be inaccurate to label blockchains as a tool for the disintermediation of trust. In reality, they only enable a re-intermediation of trust.

2. Blockchains enable a degree of trust unbundling. The blockchain challenges the roles of some existing trust players and reassigns some of their responsibilities, sometimes weakening their authority.
3. The blockchain does not eliminate trust. It shifts it. It moves it around.
4. Trust is always needed. What changes with the blockchain is how trust is delivered and how it is earned. Whoever earns the trust earns the relationship and that includes trusting a blockchain.
5. The blockchain decentralizes trust and makes way to multiple, singularly harmless, but collectively powerful entities that authenticate it.
6. The blockchain disrupts existing economics of trust because the costs of delivering that trust are now distributed.
7. Whereas central trust distanced us, distributed trust will bring us together.

This may sound abstract, but a key aspiration of blockchains is to become a dial tone for trust-based services. This means that we will be able to check and verify the veracity and authenticity of facts, data, processes, events, or anything, with the same simplicity as googling for information, services, or products today.

Dialing, or googling for trust will be possible as we perfect our iterations of "trust logic."

We already have perfected network logic. You connect your computer to the Internet and it works. You go to a Wi-Fi spot and it finds your computer. You get into your car and it connects with your smartphone via bluetooth. All this works magically because we have figured out the logic behind connecting networks and made the act of connecting seamless and easy for users.

The next logic we will need to figure out is *trust logic*. It will be about embedding trust inside hardware or software systems, and enabling the products and services behind these connections to easily interact with one another. Think about the multitude of things and offerings that can get smart when they are trusted to perform certain operations without human assistance.

Transparency and truth seeking are complementary characteristics of trust. Transparency asks the question: can we see it? Truth asks: can we verify it?

HOW AIRBNB DESIGNED TRUST FOR STRANGERS

What does Airbnb have to do with blockchain-based trust? *A lot.*

There is a lesson from Airbnb, which has mastered the art of allowing strangers to sleep in your house without fear. At the onset, matching two strangers with each other and facilitating a transaction to completion is very similar to a blockchain facilitating peer-to-peer interaction between two (or more) parties that do not know each other.

What is common to both situations is what lubricates the transaction and allows it to happen in an orderly and trustworthy manner. That common element is about sharing identity and reputation details. In the case of Airbnb, guests share a lot of information about themselves—a key step that helps the host in gaining confidence about trusting them. On the blockchain, identity and reputation are the primary entry-level factors that effectively lock the peer-to-peer transaction in place.

Says Joe Gebbia, Airbnb co-founder, "It turns out, a well-designed reputation system is key for building trust. We also learned that building the right amount of trust takes the right amount of disclosure."

Whereas Airbnb has designed for the human element of trust, the blockchain was designed for a parallel element of transactional trust, where the human is also part of it, but behind the scenes, and that human is represented on the blockchain via their identity and reputation status.

Eventually, Airbnb could also apply a user's blockchain identity and reputation to complement their current reputation and identification process. Why reinvent something if the blockchain provides a solid alternative that is portable to other services?

A SPECTRUM OF TRUST SERVICES BASED ON PROOFS

The burden of proving that something happened is a blockchain specialty. The hierarchy of proof methods range from being embedded as part of a consensus protocol (such as Proof-of-Work or Proof-of-Stake), to Proof-as-a-Service (such as proving an identity or ownership), to a Proof-in-the-Service, where proving something is part of another service (such as a land registry or a wedding registration).

THE PROOFS PYRAMID

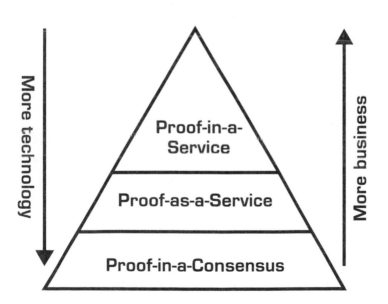

Here is a table that covers some examples of proof-related services in the different segments where we might encounter them. We can expect a long list of innovations in the Proof-in-a-Service and Proof-as-a-Service categories.

PROOF-IN-A-SERVICE	
• Wedding registry	• Counterparty transactions
• Land registry	• Accounting audits
• Supply chains	• Voting
• Asset registrations	• Deed transfer

PROOF-AS-A-SERVICE	
• Proof of asset	• Proof of ownership
• Proof of identity	• Proof of physical address
• Proof of authenticity	• Proof of provenance
• Proof of individuality	• Proof of receipt

PROOF-IN-A-CONSENSUS	
• Proof of work	• Proof of authority
• Proof of stake	• Proof of existence

THE BLOCKCHAIN LANDSCAPE

One way to understand how the blockchain market will evolve is by portraying it according to three successive layers of architecture. I've again borrowed from a popular segmentation method I used in the late 1990s to explain the Internet:

- Infrastructure and Protocols
- Middleware and Services
- End-User Applications

Generically, the narrative goes like this. First, you need a strong set of infrastructure capabilities as foundational elements. For the Internet, it was TCP/IP, HTTP, SMTP, as examples of building blocks. For the blockchain, it will be the different flavors of blockchain protocols being laid out as infrastructure. Then, you need a number of middleware software and services that will be built or delivered on top of the infrastructure elements. Middleware extends the functionality of the infrastructure elements, and makes it easier to build applications. It is like the glue between the infrastructure and applications. Finally, thousands of applications will flourish by relying on the infrastructure and middleware software and services, because they are being built on top of them.

Ideally, the more mature the bottom two layers are, the easier the development of applications becomes. As far as evolution goes, these three layers do not get created in a clear-cut order of succession. Developers start to build applications even when the infrastructure and middleware layers are not completely built out. Then, everything progresses via an iterative evolution, in each of the various layers of this landscape depiction.

BENEFITS AND INDIRECT BENEFITS

So, what are the benefits of blockchain technology? What problems does it solve?

Entrepreneurs and startups do not need to ask. They have taken to this new technology like ducks to water and are busy creating new businesses and solutions that want to replace existing ones, using different rules.

Enterprises are the ones asking, because the benefits are not necessarily obvious to them. For large companies, the blockchain presented itself as a headache initially. It was something they had not planned for.

Here's the sad truth about questioning the blockchain's benefits: if you are content with the status quo, then you will think that the blockchain does not add any value. True, the blockchain is not for everything, but if it were for something you are protecting, and you ignore the blockchain, then one day, you might realize your judgment error when a blockchain-based company starts to affect your existing business.

The blockchain may have suffered initially from the fortune cookie principle, as outlined by Bernadette Jiwa:[1] "People do not buy fortune cookies because they taste better than every other cookie on the shelf. They buy them for the delight they deliver at the end of a meal. Marketers spend most of their time selling the cookie, when what they should be doing is finding a way to create a better fortune. Of course your job is to bake a good cookie, the very best that you can, but you must also spend time figuring out how to tell a great story."

For developers, the blockchain has meaning. They have found the fortune story inside, before eating the cookie. But for the general public of users and many enterprises, Bitcoin, blockchains or cryptocurrencies do not have a lot a meaning (yet), because they are being sold the cookie.

Engineers typically want to solve a technical problem. But if solving the technical problem does not result in solving an end-user problem, users will ask: "Was that a solution looking for a problem…because I do not see this problem."

The end-user mindset just wants a simple solution to work. The end-user does not care who created or who dreamt a particular technological novelty. Business stakeholders are also part of this equation, because they know that problems cost them money, and they welcome the solutions that address these problems.

Generically, the blockchain's benefits can be examined on a long list:

- *Cost savings:* direct or indirect.
- *Speed:* removing time delays.

- **Transparency:** providing the right information to the right people.
- **Better privacy:** protecting consumers, businesses via more granular controls.
- **Lower risk:** better visibility, less exposure, less fraud, less tampering.
- **Access:** more equitable access.
- **Productivity:** more work output.
- **Efficiency:** faster processing or reporting.
- **Quality:** less errors or more satisfaction.
- **Outcomes:** profits and growth.

Blockchain is not a process improvement type of technology, but it will get used for that, because it's easier to improve an existing process than to invent a new one. At least, that is the conventional wisdom, and prevailing *modus operandi* within large organizations.

Yes, you can improve by 1.5x or 2x and that's a respectable achievement, but what if you could improve by 10x?

There is a strange dichotomy between how startups and large companies see blockchains. Startups see it as a solution to everything, whereas big companies see it as a pain, since it challenges existing processes.

EXPLAINING SOME BASIC FUNCTIONS

Smart Property

Smart property is a native unit requirement for blockchain operations. To understand it, think of its two predecessors, a "digital file" and a "digital asset." A digital asset is a digitized version of a product that includes specific rights to use, and typically has a value attached to it. Without rights, it is not considered to be an asset, and is just a "digital file." Examples of a digital asset include a song, an e-book, a photo, or a logo. Prior to the Bitcoin invention, it did not make sense to have money as a digital asset, because the double-spend (or double-send) problem was not solved yet, which meant that fraud could have dominated. As a parallel, when you send a photo from your smartphone to someone, you still maintain a copy, and you are both owners of that image. That would not be acceptable in the money world, or with assets that are of real value or right, and cannot be shared with multiple owners.

Smart property takes the concept of a digital asset further, and it links the asset to a blockchain such that it can never be double-spent, double-owned or double-sent. If you are a creator or owner of these digital assets, imagine if you could also bind your ownership (or rights) in irrevocable ways that cannot be undone unless you decide to transfer or sell them. And it's all within your own control, not someone else's.

As such, you would be creating a smart property, which is an asset or thing that knows who owns it. A smart property does not have to be a digital-only product. It can be a physical object or thing that was made "smart" through an explicit or implicit linkage to a blockchain. There are thousands of such examples, including a lock, a car, a fridge, or even your house. The blockchain can be used as an auditable database linked to your cryptographic signature, and your smart property becomes linked to a unique digital fingerprint based on its content.

Now imagine the portability, flexibility, and discoverability aspects that accompany these capabilities, and they become a great lubricator for decentralized peer-to-peer transactions, financial trading or commerce. A smart property is the new form of digital bits that are made for the blockchain rails.

Timestamping
Timestamping is a basic function that permanently registers on the blockchain the time that a particular action took place. For example, this could be the recording of an asset's change of ownership,

or the fact that an action occurred, like a medical exam or a specific transaction. This is useful to prove or verify at a later date that an event actually took place at that particular time. Timestamping is an irrefutable and immutable action once recorded on a blockchain, so it is useful when seeking the truth.

Multisignature Transactions

Multisignature (also known as multisig) is a process where more than one signature is required to clear the status of a transaction or to give the go-ahead for an approval. It is the equivalent of requiring multiple signatures on a paper agreement to make it valid, but this happens automatically and quickly on the blockchain. What makes this approach even more powerful is that you can insert business logic in-between the multiple signatures, so that each signature can trigger a new action, resulting in the creation of escrow services as part of these transactions.

Smart Contracts

Smart contracts are a key underpinning of blockchain technology. If you do not understand smart contracts, then you do not understand the power of blockchains. They will be no less revolutionary than the invention of the HTML markup language that allowed information to be openly published and linked on the Web. Smart contracts promise to program our world on the head of blockchains, and potentially replace some of the functions currently executed by expensive or slow, legacy intermediaries.

The concept was first introduced by Nick Szabo in 1994,[2] but it underwent a long gestation period of inactivity and disinterest, because there was no platform that could enforce smart contracts, until the advent of the Bitcoin blockchain technology in 2009. Since 2015, smart contracts have been gaining popularity, especially since Ethereum made programming them a basic tenet of their blockchain's power.

Like any new buzzword, the more a term gets popular, the more it spreads around, and the more it will get used, but also misused and abused. It will mean a lot of different things to different people. Here are some facts about smart contracts:

1. **Smart contracts are not the same as a contractual agreement.** If we stick to Nick Szabo's original idea, smart contracts help make the breach of an agreement expensive because they control a real-world valuable property via "digital means." So, a smart contract can enforce a functional implementation of a particular requirement, and can show proof that certain conditions were met or not met. These can be fairly strict implementations, for example, if a car payment is not made on-time, the car gets digitally locked until the payment is received.

2. **Smart contracts are not like Ricardian contracts.** Ricardian contracts, popularized by Ian Grigg,[3] are semantic representations that can track the liability of an actual agreement between parties. These can also be implemented on a blockchain, with or without a smart contract. Typically, multisignatures are part of a Ricardian contract's execution.

3. **Smart contracts are not law.** Smart contracts, being computer programs, are just the enabling technology, but the consequence of their actions can be made part of a legal agreement, for example a smart contract could transfer shares ownerships from one party to another. As of 2016, the full legal ramifications around smart contracts were a work in progress. A smart contract outcome could be used as an audit trail to prove if terms of legal agreement were followed or not.

4. **Smart contracts do not include Artificial Intelligence.** Smart contracts are software code representing business

logic that runs a blockchain, and they are triggered by some external data that lets them modify some other data. They are closer to an event-driven construct, more than artificial intelligence.

5. **Smart contracts are not the same as blockchain applications.** Smart contracts are usually part of a decentralized (blockchain) application. There could be several contracts to a specific application. For example, if certain conditions in a smart contract are met, then the program is allowed to update a database.

6. **Smart contracts are fairly easy to program.** Writing a simple contract is easy, especially if you are using a specific smart contract language (e.g., Ethereum's Solidity), which lets you write complex processes in a few lines of code. But there are more advanced implementations of smart contracts that use "oracles." Oracles are data sources that send actionable information to smart contracts.

7. **Smart contracts are not for developers only.** The next generation of smart contracts will include user-friendly entry points, like a Web browser. That will allow any business user to configure smart contracts via a graphical user interface, or perhaps a text-based language input.

8. **Smart contracts are safe.** Even in the Ethereum implementation, smart contracts run as quasi-Turing complete programs. This means there is finality in their execution, and they do not risk looping infinitely.

9. **Smart contract have a wide range of applications.** Like HTML, the applications are limited by whoever writes them. Smart contracts are ideal for interacting with real-world assets, smart property, Internet of Things (IoT), and financial services instruments. They are not limited to money movements. They apply to almost anything that changes its state over time, and could have a value attached to it.

Developers with smart contracts expertise will be in demand. Learning smart contracts allows one to get into blockchains, without the burden of getting directly under the hood of blockchains. Many smart contract languages are derivatives of C++, Java or Python, three of the most popular software languages, and that makes learning them a lot easier.

Smart contracts are an under-appreciated piece of blockchain technology architecture. Yet, they promise to power the blockchains of the future.

If trust is the atomic unit of blockchains, then smart contracts are what programs the variety of trust into specific applications. Soon enough, there will be millions of smart contracts bombarding blockchains with logical representations of our world, and that will be a good evolution to expect.

Smart Oracles

Oracles are an interesting concept, relating to smart contracts. You can think of them as off-chain data sources that a smart contract can use to modify its behavior. Smart oracles contain a real-world representation of information, such as an identity, an address, or a certificate, and they could also have agent-like property that directs the smart contract to behave in a certain way.

They work together in harmony because one of them is on the blockchain (smart contracts), and the other one is off-chain (smart oracles). For example, a smart contract that concerns itself with a Know Your Customer (KYC) function could interact with a smart oracle that contains identity information. Or, if a police officer wishes to check the status of a driver's license, instead of dialing the motor vehicle database, they could check the blockchain and get the latest information pertaining to the validity of the license, its expiry, or other driver-related information. Conceivably, instead of maintaining expensive central databases, the motor vehicle department could become a smart oracle and publish their data on the blockchain. The data would be encrypted, and only accessible to authorities that hold the right keys to access them, but the process would be more efficient and less costly to maintain.[4]

WHAT DOES A TRUSTED BLOCKCHAIN ENABLE?

I have suggested a practical way to remember what the blockchain touches. Just think of the word ATOMIC, and you will remember what each letter means:

Assets, Trust, Ownership, Money, Identity, Contracts

Indeed, the blockchain offers:

- Programmable *Assets*
- Programmable *Trust*
- Programmable *Ownership*
- Programmable *Money*
- Programmable *Identity*
- Programmable *Contracts*

Put together, these six concepts are powerful catalysts for understanding where the blockchain can be used in any particular situation.

Let us expand on some of these topics.

Creation and Real-Time Movement of Digital Assets

Digital assets can be created, managed, and transferred on a blockchain network without incurring clearing-related delays due to the existence of intermediaries. Not requiring human or central database intervention to enforce verifiability is a fundamental novelty.

Embedding Trust Rules Inside Transactions & Interactions

By inserting rules that represent trust inside transactions, the blockchain becomes a new way to validate these transactions via logic in the network, not via a database entry or central authority. Therefore, a new "trust factor" is created that is part of the transaction itself.

Time-Stamping, Rights, & Ownership Proofs
The blockchain allows the time-stamping of documents representing rights or ownerships, therefore providing irrefutable proofs that are cryptographically secure. This, in turn, can enable a variety of applications to be built on top of these new seamless verification capabilities.

Self-Execution of Business Logic with Self-Enforcement
Because verification is done by the blockchain's black box, and the trust component is part of the transaction, the end-result is a self-clearing transaction. The clearing and settlement of assets are merged together.

Selective Transparency & Privacy
This is achieved via cryptographic technologies, and it will result in new levels of decentralized data privacy and security where transactions can be verified without revealing everything about the identity of their owners. Transparency exposes the ethics of a business, so it will get resisted. But increased transparency can also provide increased levels of trust.

Resistance to Single Points of Failure or Censorship
Because the blockchain consists of several decentralized computers and resources, there is no single point of failure; therefore, the network is more resilient than centrally controlled infrastructures. Blockchains are typically censorship resistant, due to the decentralized nature of data storage, encryption, and peer controls at the edge of the network.

IDENTITY OWNERSHIPS & REPRESENTATION

Anonymous, pseudonymous, or real identities can be uniquely mapped on the blockchain, offering us the promise of owning our own identities, and not having them controlled by Google or Facebook.

The vision of blockchain-based identity promises to empower users to be in complete control of their identity.

This promise could lead to easy, single, or seamless sign-ons that zigzag Internet users straight through the maze of entry and access points to unlock personal information, access services, and transact with digital assets.

In its simplest form, the blockchain can be used to uniquely authenticate your identification, in irrefutable and immutable ways, because your "keys" are your identity. But what happens if you need several keys instead of just one, because every service you use requires a different one? Imagine if you had five keys to your house, and depending on the day, or the entry point, you'd need to use a different one. Or, if you had five different homes in different parts of the world, you would certainly come up with a way to keep your keys. It's definitely possible, but burdensome.

Online, we are already challenged by keeping track of multiple passwords in our heads, or in notes, and we're always worried about getting hacked potentially, or forgetting them. I would expect that blockchain-assisted identity and access solutions can help us arrive at better solutions than the current ones.

In an ideal world, why couldn't our online and offline identities blur? Why do we accept that our driver's license is only valid in physical settings (mostly), and our online identities (Facebook or other) are useless at airport security or at the bank? Of course, newly issued passports are beginning to bridge that divide when we scan them at the airport kiosks, and we complete our identification via a retinal scan, or other pieces of information to triangulate on our identity.

In the blockchain world, there are various approaches that are addressing identity and personal security, including granting us access to data and services. Some require new hardware solutions, others are software-based, and some integrate with business-to-business solutions.

Hardware. The analogy is similar to showing a passport, or other government-issued identity card, such as a driver's license. That card gives us access to travel, or authorizes us to drive a car. On the blockchain, some of these solutions are also combining biometric data to add to the authentication mix. Examples: ShoCard, Case.

Software. The closest analogy is the current OAuth-based identifications we routinely perform on the Web when signing into websites using our Facebook, Twitter or Google IDs. But with blockchain solutions, the roles are reversed: you self-register your identity first, and then you link to your social accounts. Examples: Netki, OneName, BitID, Identifi.

Integration-first. Whereas the first two approaches generally start with the consumer, this segment starts by figuring out the integration requirements with existing business solutions. Examples: Cambridge Blockchain, Trunomi, uPort, Tradle, Ripple KYC Gateway.

Blockchain identification schemes have a chance, but there are uncertainties ahead. On the consumer side, could they replace our linking to Facebook, Google, or Twitter, and lure us to start with them instead? And on the business side, could they supplant already entrenched solutions such as SWIFT's 3SKey multi-bank, multi-network personal identity solution, or Markit's KYC?

For blockchain-based solutions, the bar is high for simplicity requirements and reaching large numbers of users. They are going against the millions of Google, Facebook, and Twitter users, or the thousands of financial institutions already using SWIFT or Markit.

Of course the blockchain industry could have its own solution. Why should we be subjected to repetitive Know Your Customer processes each time we register for a new cryptocurrency exchange? Let us not make the same mistake as in the physical world.

When it comes to the implementation and evolution of blockchain solutions, there are a few issues and questions:

Consumer Questions

What sorts of applications will drive these new forms of identity representations? In the Facebook and Google world, their specific application (e.g., social media or documents access) drives our usage. But on the blockchain, most identity solutions providers are rushing to deliver solutions before bolting them onto applications that will drive usage.

- Can a self-managed online personal identity layer supplant the current de-facto standard of using Facebook or Google to authenticate our identity and information access?
- Will users be willing to self-manage the complexity that comes with higher levels of security rules and access levels?
- What does portability really mean in the context of identity? Will it lead to managing multiple identities, and will that become a similar nightmare as managing passwords?
- What is the role of zero knowledge technology to protect the confidentiality of transactions and the privacy of individuals?
- What is the role of the smartphone? Can it become our "digital passport," as it is already becoming our digital wallet?

Business Considerations

What happens if we lose our secured card or private keys? Can the average user be trusted to self-manage access to their data in the same ease as protecting one's own property at home, for example?

- Do we need new types of certificate authorities to provide their stamps of approvals on these identity systems?
- Could we configure information access in more granular ways, so that peer-to-peer security rules can supplant firewall-based solutions?
- What is the relationship with current Know Your Customer (KYC) practices, and will these new identity solutions provide a more secure layer for facilitating AML and counterterrorism types of activities?
- Will this drive more consumer or business applications?
- Are there legal or regulatory hurdles that need to be addressed to enable the full deployment of these types of solutions?

Ethical Questions

Changing habits is one of the biggest hurdles to technology adoption, and this area is no different. We do not know yet if a full move to digital identities would invite some abuse, or decrease friction, and increase total user engagement.

- Is the separation of data and identity a good thing? Does it create multiple pseudo identities and personas ad nauseam?
- How about the impact of transaction history on our reputation? Will rating our online reputation become the new consumer credit score equivalent?
- Is anonymity a good thing, or can that moniker be abused to achieve malicious goals?
- Does this open up the market to promote financial inclusion, or does it raise the adoption bar higher?

DECENTRALIZED DATA SECURITY

The blockchain brings some solutions to the dilemma of balancing data, identity, and transaction-based privacy and security.

We have seen security and privacy breaches within large/central organizations (for example, Target, Sony, Blue Cross, Ashley Madison, and the Turkish government), and that is leading us to wonder if the Web or large databases are really secure anymore. The privacy of customer information, citizens, and transaction history can be compromised, and this has implications on the security of applications data and online identities.

Enter the blockchain and decentralized applications based on it. Their advent brings potential solutions to data security because cryptographically-secured encryption becomes a standard part of blockchain applications, especially pertaining to the data parts. By default, everything is encrypted. By virtue of decentralizing the information architecture elements, each user can own their private data, and central repositories are less vulnerable to data losses or breaches because they only store encrypted information and coded pointers to distributed storage locations that are spread across distributed computer networks. Therefore, hackers cannot reconstruct or make sense of whatever partial information they might get their hands on. At least, that's the theory behind this vision, and work is being done to bring it to reality.

In this new world of decentralized technologies, security, privacy, and data ownership requirements are part of the design and not an afterthought. They come first.

But blockchains are not perfect. They also introduce security challenges due to their inherent designs relating to three key areas:

- Consensus engines on blockchains
- Decentralization of computing architectures
- Peer-to-peer clients

Consensus in public blockchains is done publicly, and is theoretically subject to the proverbial Sybil attacks (although it has not happened yet). The trend for decentralized computing architectures requires a new mindset for planning and writing applications that is different than the traditional Web architectures. Finally, each time you download a software client that sits on your personal computer or smartphone and it "listens" to the network, you are potentially opening security risks, unless it is well implemented.

We also need to be aware that Internet of Things devices also are subject to potential security breaches, because potential vulnerabilities are being pushed from the centers to the edges, wherever there is some computing resources at the edge.

Luckily, some solutions are in the works, such as private blockchains, zero-knowledge proofs and ring signatures, but we will not enter this technical territory within the scope of this book.

Another bright light is that we do not need to reinvent decentralized security, decentralized data and how to write decentralized applications because there are new platforms that provide these basic buildings blocks as part of their core offerings.

If you are a developer, the implications for the future are to:

1. Secure data inside applications while you write them
2. Decentralize user data to protect it
3. Learn blockchains and decentralization technologies
4. Write smart contracts on new/thin cloud architectures (no servers)
5. Rethink identity ownerships for your customers

Security and privacy need to be part of the initial design, and not as an afterthought.

ANONYMITY & UNTRACEABLE COMMUNICATION

The blockchain enables user anonymity by choice, and it is one of the most annoying features for regulators and financial reporting authorities, specifically in consumer applications. What comes to their mind, of course, would be money laundering, illicit trade, and terrorism-related activities where users could hide under pseudo-anonymous identities, and stay under the radar for a long time before they get discovered. Obviously, this is not a design objective of public blockchains or decentralized applications that run them, and although they are corner cases for the normal person, they can be seen as show-stoppers for policy makers and government institutions.

Without brushing aside the potential risks associated with implicitly protecting criminals and bad actors, there are cases where untraceable communication is desirable, for good and valid reasons.

Says David Shaum, the inventor of digital cash and privacy technologies: "Untraceable communication is fundamental to freedom of inquiry, freedom of expression, and increasingly to online privacy generally, including person-to-person communication. To address these needs a system should support, ideally within a combined anonymity set, the most common use cases: chat, photo/video sharing, feed following, searching, posting, payments, all with various types of potentially pseudonymous authentication."

In 1994, Kevin Kelly, author of *Out of Control*, wrote this:

A pretty good society needs more than just anonymity. An online civilization requires online anonymity, online identification, online authentication, online reputations, online trust holders, online signatures, online privacy, and online access. All are essential ingredients of any open society.

It is disheartening to realize that, as of 2016, we were still very much behind on that vision of a "pretty good, open, online society." The blockchain can help, because too many Web companies centralized and hijacked what could have been a more decentralized set of services.

There is hope that we can reconcile the anonymity and accountability requirements, and strike a good balance between the two, where "evil doers" can be rooted out of the network, while preserving the normality of operations for the majority of "good" users.[5]

BLOCKCHAIN AS CLOUD

We can also think of blockchains as a shared infrastructure that is like a utility. If you think about how the current Internet infrastructure is being paid for, we subsidize it by paying monthly fees to Internet service providers. As public blockchains proliferate and we start running millions of smart contracts and verification services on them, we might be also subsidizing their operations, by paying via micro transactions, in the form of transaction fees, smart contracts tolls, donation buttons, or pay-per-use schemes.

Blockchains are like a remote computer somewhere in a distributed cloud that is virtual and does not require server setups. Whoever opens a blockchain node runs the server, but not users or developers.

So, the blockchain is like a networked infrastructure of computing machinery. With that in mind, we could easily imagine how computer programs can run on this new infrastructure.

But we should not take the cloud computing analogy literally. The blockchain infrastructure does not replace cloud computing. It unbundles it, and democratizes parts of it.

More likely, the blockchain infrastructure resembles a layer of cloud computing infrastructure. Blockchain virtual machines may be too expensive if we are to literally compare their functionality to a typical cloud service such as Amazon Web Services or DigitalOcean, but they will be be certainly useful for smart contracts that execute their logic on the blockchain's virtual machinery, or decentralized applications, also called Dapps. As a sidenote, we could also see a future where client nodes can talk to each other directly in scenarios where blockchains are too expensive or slow.

When you run an application in the cloud (for example, on Amazon Web Services or Microsoft Azure), you are billed according to a combination of time, storage, data transfer, and computing speed requirements. The novelty with virtual machine costing is that you are paying to run the business logic on the blockchain, which is otherwise running on physical servers (on existing cloud infrastructure), but you do not have to worry about setting up these servers because they are managed by other users who are getting paid anyways for running that infrastructure via mining.

Therefore, the blockchain cloud has a form of micro-value pricing model that parallels the traditional cloud computing stack, but via a new layer. It is not a physical unbundling of the cloud, rather it is a new layering of cryptography-based transaction validation and state transition recordings on a parallel, but thinner cloud.

But here is the challenge to running applications on this new infrastructure: you need to do some work. That work comes in the form of adhering to a new paradigm of decentralized apps that follows a new tiered architecture coined as "web3" by Gavin Wood.[6] Web3 is an architecture that runs specifically on the blockchain. Using Ethereum as a primary example, a web3 architecture includes: 1) an advanced browser as the client, 2) the blockchain ledger as a shared resource, and 3) a virtual network of computers that runs smart business logic programs in a decentralized way by interacting with the blockchain consensus engine that clears transactions or toggles some value. This new paradigm actually exemplifies the future direction of cryptography-based decentralized computing. It is a variation of the existing Web apps architecture consisting of running Javascript inside browsers and server-side code that is run on company servers.

What is happening here within a grander context? Let us put this in perspective. We are witnessing a delayering across various technology pieces:

- Applications Programming Interfaces (APIs) are now coming from a public infrastructure that is cryptographically secured (the blockchains).
- Blockchains are being used as a new form of database, for example as a place to permanently store immutable cryptographic keys (or hashes) in Distributed Hash Tables (DHTs) that point to larger data values that are stored off-chain.
- A new type of browser will allow users to launch decentralized apps (Dapps), not just Web pages (e.g., Mist from Ethereum).
- The World Wide Web's original Hypertext Protocol is getting augmented by a new hypermedia protocol called InterPlanetary File System (IPFS), which is a peer-to-peer distributed file system that connects all computing devices with the same system of files.
- Contractual Law is being sliced off, for example via Ricardian contracts that track the liability of one party to another (for example, OpenBazaar is implementing them in their peer-to-peer e-commerce protocol).

Here is a profound implication for large enterprises. Business users will also be able to run their own smart contracts, P2P apps, and other Dapps on open blockchains without seeking permission from IT departments, in the same way that Software-as-a-Service (SaaS) was a Trojan horse that enabled employees to sign up for services on their own without disturbing the company infrastructures (until it was time to perform some integrations).

This new form of SaaS will be possible because a new infrastructure layer can emerge by being supported on a peer-to-peer and shared-cost basis. And it is very possible that the costs of this new computing infrastructure will be as cheap as Internet access today, on a relative per-user basis. If that's the case, this expands the applications possibilities even further.

The thin cloud represents freedom and flexibility for users and developers. It will allow anyone to create their own business logic for ownership, commerce, contractual law, transaction formats, and state transition functions without worrying about setting up an infrastructure.

We must fully embrace the thin cloud as an outcome of the blockchains' infrastructures, and we must innovate with creative applications that run on it.

GETTING TO MILLIONS OF BLOCKCHAINS

In 1994, when the Web came along, websites were the novelty, and up until about 1998, we kept lists of Fortune 500 companies with or without websites. It took about three years before most companies were on board. Then, many of these early sites were criticized for being mostly glorified brochures or information sheets, and we kept referring to Amazon as one of the few companies that actually conducted business on the Internet.

Fast forward to 2016 and beyond. The blockchain will be the new website, figuratively speaking. Yes, blockchains are geeky (and the challenge is to take out that geekiness), but every company is destined to own or participate in a variety of blockchains, whether they are private, semi-private, or public.

Using the website analogy, companies could use the familiar portal approach to deliver a range of blockchain services, to facilitate the on-boarding of new users, while showcasing the blockchain's capabilities.

The first steps involve finding what is appropriate for the

blockchain, starting with your current operations. Just as with your first website when the question was, "What information can we publish on it?," there are initial questions you can try answering first, to uncover potential blockchain use cases pertaining to the variety of peer-to-peer value exchange services that are possible.

It is almost unimaginable to think that when Satoshi Nakamoto released the code for the first Bitcoin blockchain in 2009, it consisted of just two computers and a token. Then, it proceeded to grow because anyone could download a software program and connect to the network as another identical node that ran the same code. It proceeded to become a self-growing type of network. That is how public blockchains grow.

Bitcoin was that first public blockchain, and it inspired many others. Ethereum was another major public blockchain that has grown rapidly to establish itself as the second largest and significant public, multi-purpose blockchain.

One of the primary differences between a public and private blockchain is that public blockchains typically have a generic purpose and are generally cheaper to use, whereas private blockchains have a more specific usage, and they are more expensive to set up because the cost is born by fewer owners. We can also expect special purpose public blockchains to emerge, for example, the Zcash one that promises to deliver total privacy.

With the proliferation of public, private, semi-private, special purpose, and other types of blockchains, a world of millions of blockchains will be achievable.

KEY IDEAS FROM CHAPTER TWO

1. Blockchains offer a new paradigm for implementing transactional trust. We should open our minds, and accept that trust will be computed by machines, instead of verified by humans.

2. Trust can be achieved by increasing transparency requirements, namely by sharing identity and reputation information.

3. Proving that something has happened will be served by blockchains. There will be millions of such cases, with access rivalling the way we google for information.

4. Anonymity, identity, decentralized data, and security are evolving issues that are well suited for blockchains.

5. Smart contracts and smart property are key underpinnings of a blockchain's operations, as they open up the applications, possibilities. Developers will rush to create smart contract-based applications without worrying about learning the internal elements of blockchains.

NOTES

1. "The Fortune Cookie Principle™," Bernadette Jiwa, http://thestoryoftelling.com/fortune-cookie-principle/.

2. Smart Contracts, Nick Szabo, http://szabo.best.vwh.net/smart_contracts_idea.html.

3. The Ricardian Contract, Ian Grigg, http://iang.org/papers/ricardian_contract.html.

4. Digital Identity on Blockchain: Alex Batlin's "prediction," Alex Batlin,http://fintechnews.ch/803/blockchain_bitcoin/digital-identity-on-blockchain-alex-batlins-prediction/.

5. PrivaTegrity—David Chaum's Anonymous Communications Project, SecurityWeek, http://www.securityweek.com/privategrity-david-chaums-anonymous-communications-project.

6. Less-techy: What is Web 3.0, Gavin Wood, http://gavwood.com/web3lt.html.

□-□-3-□-□

OBSTACLES, CHALLENGES, & MENTAL BLOCKS

"When the wind of change blows, some people build walls, others build windmills."

—CHINESE PROVERB

ONCE, a youth went to see a wise man, and said to him:

"I have come seeking advice, for I am tormented by feelings of worthlessness and no longer wish to live. Everyone tells me that I am a failure and a fool. I beg you, Master, help me!"

The wise man glanced at the youth, and answered hurriedly: "Forgive me, but I am very busy right now and cannot help you. There is one urgent matter in particular which I need to attend to..."—and here he stopped, for a moment, thinking, then added: "But if you agree to help me, I will happily return the favor."

"Of...of course, Master!" muttered the youth, noting bitterly that yet again his concerns had been dismissed as unimportant. "Good," said the wise man, and took off a small ring with a beautiful gem from his finger.

"Take my horse and go to the market square! I urgently need to sell this ring in order to pay off a debt. Try to get a decent price for

it, and do not settle for anything less than one gold coin! Go right now, and come back as quick as you can!"

The youth took the ring and galloped off. When he arrived at the market square, he showed it to the various traders, who at first examined it with close interest. But no sooner had they heard that it would sell only in exchange for gold than they completely lost interest. Some of the traders laughed openly at the boy; others simply turned away. Only one aged merchant was decent enough to explain to him that a gold coin was too high a price to pay for such a ring, and that he was more likely to be offered only copper, or at best, possibly silver.

When he heard these words, the youth became very upset, for he remembered the old man's instruction not to accept anything less than gold. Having already gone through the whole market looking for a buyer among hundreds of people, he saddled the horse and set off. Feeling thoroughly depressed by his failure, he returned to see the wise man.

"Master, I was unable to carry out your request," he said. "At best I would have been able to get a couple of silver coins, but you told me not to agree to anything less than gold! But they told me that this ring is not worth that much."

"That's a very important point, my boy!" the wise man responded. "Before trying to sell a ring, it would not be a bad idea to establish how valuable it really is! And who can do that better than a jeweler? Ride over to him and find out what his price is. Only do not sell it to him, regardless of what he offers you! Instead, come back to me straightaway."

The young man once more leapt up on to the horse and set off to see the jeweler. The latter examined the ring through a magnifying glass for a long time, then weighed it on a set of tiny scales. Finally, he turned to the youth and said:

"Tell your master that right now I cannot give him more than 58 gold coins for it. But if he gives me some time, I will buy the ring for 70."

"70 gold coins?!" exclaimed the youth. He laughed, thanked the jeweler and rushed back at full speed to the wise man. When the latter heard the story from the now animated youth, he told him: "Remember, my boy, that you are like this ring. Precious, and unique! And only a real expert can appreciate your true value. So why are you wasting your time wandering through the market and heeding the opinion of any old fool?"

This parable reminds of the fits and trials of Bitcoin, cryptocurrencies and blockchain technologies. Along their journey to gain legitimacy and be recognized, they have confronted plenty of skepticism and lower than deserved valuations, mostly during encounters with the part of the audience that could not fully appreciate their real worth.

The blockchain will meet resistance, be misunderstood and rejected, until it is widely accepted. This is a somber chapter in this book. If you read it on its own, you might decide that the blockchain will never succeed. Hopefully, you will not sell it short at the "market of fools," like the above tale suggested.

Yes, there are plenty of challenges and unknowns, but we had similar blind spots and uncertainties during the early years of the Internet, from 1994 to 1998. Fast forward 15 to 20 years later, perceptions changed about the Internet. It became commonly accepted that almost nothing would be impossible with it. Pick anything. There is probably a Web-related solution or option for it, yet this level of market penetration was unthinkable during the early years.

Blockchains today are equally full of excitement and skepticism. The Internet turned out to be a wonderful tool, because the excited groups won over the skeptics. But that didn't occur by happenstance, sheer enthusiasm, or just the passage of time. It happened because, early on, market participants were able to identify the challenges to the Internet's commercialization, and one by one, they were tackled, such that the barriers of entry kept getting smaller and lower, and the opportunities became larger and more reachable.

I saw this up close with the Internet, around 1994, having participated in the advocacy of its early commercialization, through my affiliation with CommerceNet. Its sole purpose was to help remove the barriers to adoption, evangelize its vision, and expose its benefits, by working on technological, educational, legal and regulatory initiatives that lubricated the Internet's early development days. The blockchain's evolution will repeat the Internet's history, undoubtedly.

ATTACKING THE BLOCKCHAIN WITH A FRAMEWORK APPROACH

Let us look at the blockchain holistically through the lens of a Catalyst-Barrier-Solution framework perspective. This framework consists of accurately depicting the catalysts: business drivers and technology enablers. Then, we can table the barriers that include technical, business/market, legal/regulatory, and behavioral/educational challenges. Finally, we have a responsibility to tackle the solutions to each one of these barriers, one by one.

There should not be any illusion about the reality needed here. If we ignore the issues behind these barriers, many of them will not get solved on their own, nor will they go away, but we need to keep moving progress in the right direction.

The message behind this framework is to help us focus on what's important. Progress happens when business drivers are strong, when technology enablers are ready, and when solutions to challenges are found.

A FRAMEWORK FOR FOCUSING
BLOCKCHAIN'S SUCCESS

BUSINESS DRIVERS	TECHNOLOGY ENABLERS
Technical Challenges	Behavioral/ Educational Challenges
Market/ Business Challenges	Legal/ Regulatory Challenges

SOLUTIONS (to Barriers)

Here's a table of these challenges, categorized into four sections.

TECHNICAL	MARKET/BUSINESS
• Underdeveloped ecosystem infrastructure • Lack of mature applications • Scarcity in developers • Immature middleware and tools • Scalability • Legacy systems • Tradeoffs with databases • Privacy • Security • Lack of standards	• Moving assets to the blockchain • Quality of project ideas • Critical mass of users • Quality of startups • Venture capital • Volatility of cryptocurrency • Onboarding new users • Few poster applications companies • Not enough qualified individuals • Costs issues • Innovators dilemma[1]
BEHAVIORAL/EDUCATIONAL	**LEGAL/REGULATORY**
• Lack of understanding of potential value • Limited executive vision • Change management • Trusting a network • Few best practices • Low usability factor	• Unclear regulations • Government interferences • Compliance requirements • Hype • Taxation and reporting

TECHNICAL CHALLENGES

Software engineers and scientists love to face technical challenges. It motivates them further to try and solve them, no matter how hard they are.

Underdeveloped Ecosystem Infrastructure

As a starting point, each blockchain needs its own technology infrastructure, as well as a vibrant ecosystem around it, with a number of participants to support it. On the technology side, the protocol itself is a minimum requirement, and while it needs to be augmented by software tools and services to make it useful, it is the ecosystem of players around the technology that directly influences a blockchain's market progression. Without adoption, there is little impact.

Just as the whole of the Web works as an ecosystem, the blockchain ecosystem will follow the same emancipation path, resulting in a mesh of interconnected blockchains, even if in the meantime, it will feel like some pieces of the orchestra are missing.

A vibrant ecosystem includes a variety of players in each one of the following segments:

- Complete *technology stack*, including infrastructure, middleware, and software applications
- *Startups* that innovate by creating new products and forging new markets
- *Solutions and services providers* that deliver end-to-end implementation for enterprises
- *Funders and venture capital* that take risks alongside the entrepreneurs and scientists
- *Advocates*, influencers, analysts, volunteers, supporters, local communities
- *Developers and technologists* who work on core, and extended technology pieces
- *Users* who are conditioned to try products, both as consumers and enterprise customers

Lack of Mature Applications

It takes time for new applications to emerge when new foundational technology enters the scene. It took a long time before we were able to see ambitious and innovative Web applications, and many of the early ones were not that innovative, because they tried to replicate what was being done already in the real world. Nonetheless, replication is a good first step, because it allows one to gain experience when expectations are lower.

Taken as an extreme case, just about any software application could be rewritten with some blockchain and decentralization flavor into it, but that does not mean it's a good idea to do so.

Perhaps 2016 for blockchain is equivalent to 1995 in terms of where we were at that stage with the proliferation of Web applications. At that time, the Java Virtual Machine was not yet available, but when it was, it opened an avalanche of opportunities, and made it easier to create large scale Web applications. The advent of the Java computer programming language meant that Java applications could run on any Java Virtual Machine (JVM) regardless of computer architecture. Some blockchains such as Ethereum have a similar "virtual machine" capability, which allows programs to execute on the blockchain without requiring developers to be aware of the inherent computer architecture.

Another blockchain criticism is the lack of so-called "killer apps" that are supposed to light-up exponential usage among consumers. We will certainly expect visible applications as beacons to others, but there is another point of view supporting the case for several killer apps, not just one. For that later scenario, the proverbial "long tail" market characteristics would prevail.

Scarcity in Developers

Several thousands of software developers will be needed to lift all the boats. By mid-2016, there were approximately 5,000 developers dedicated to writing software for cryptocurrency, Bitcoin, or blockchains in general.[2] Perhaps another 20,000 had dabbled with some of that technology, or written front-end applications that connect to a blockchain, one way or the other. These numbers pale in comparison to 9 million worldwide Java developers (2016),[3] and about 18.5 million software developers in the world (2014).[4]

Luckily, blockchains are programmed with languages and scripts that are similar to already popular ones, such as Java, Javascript, C++, Node.js, Python, Golang, or Haskell.[5] This type of familiarity is a positive characteristic that will benefit programmers when they start to interact with blockchain technologies.

What will help improve the number of developers?

- More general market awareness about the blockchain to drive higher levels of interests.
- Popularity of certification programs, such as from the CryptoCurrency Certification Consortium (C4).[6]
- Availability of formal academic degrees that specialize in this field, such as the Master of Science in Digital Currency, offered by the University of Nicosia in Cyprus.
- Training programs by the blockchain providers.

Immature Middleware and Tools

Blockchain middleware and software tools are really important. The middleware is like the glue between blockchain infrastructure and the building of applications. Software development tools facilitate the overall software development projects.

Up until 1998, writing Web applications was not that easy, and required the manual assembly of several pieces of software together. During that time, several shortcomings plagued the deployment of Web applications, including the lack of robust transaction management and state related capabilities, scalability, deployment, applications manageability, and certainly security. Then, Netscape introduced the famous all-in-one "Netscape Application Server," an integrated suite of software capabilities that included the various requirement components and tools, out-of-the-box. That simplification was a boon for programmers who took to it like ducks to water, and started focusing on writing Web applications, instead of worrying about assembling the required pieces together and about incompatibilities. Those early Netscape days denoted the beginning of the modern Web applications architecture era, which continues up to this point.

As soon we start to see complete, out-of-the-box products that promise to simplify how to start, develop, and deploy blockchain applications, we will know that a new phase has started.

Scalability

Scalability of blockchains is an issue that will continue to be debated, especially pertaining to the public Bitcoin blockchain. The challenge behind scalability is two-fold:

1. There is typically more than a single way to scale any technology, and the blockchain is no different. Several engineers may not agree on the best method to scale something, a situation that may result in long discussions and implementation delays.
2. As of 2016, some aspects of blockchain scalability still require ongoing scientific research, because this new territory is closer to the edges of a new frontier.

Scaling technical systems is a never-ending challenge. It is a moving target, because the needs for scale evolve as you grow; therefore you do not need to solve a problem you do not have yet. You typically solve it, just ahead of being hit with a problem, at the right time. You do not design a solution for 1 million users, when you are still only serving the first 1,000.

For reference, more than 30 years after its initial invention, we are still designing and refining the Internet's own scalability. Eyeing 50 billion nodes in 2020 was not a design issue in 1983 or 1995. But now, the size of the network has grown significantly, and we have crossed a few billions users, we can more easily tackle the next scalability targets.

Scaling blockchains will not be different than the way we have continued to scale the Internet, conceptually speaking. There are plenty of smart engineers, scientists, researchers, and designers who are up to the challenge and will tackle it.

What complicates the scalability of blockchains even further is the required balance that needs to be preserved between decentralization and security. Scaling a decentralized network with an economic model that is tied to its security is a new frontier that has not been attempted before.

Legacy Systems

Typically, there are two issues relating to enterprise legacy systems:

1. Integration with existing applications.
2. Knowing what pieces to replace.

Technical integration with legacy or other applications will always be an IT implementation challenge. Therefore, it might be easier to develop use cases and projects outside of your existing systems, because you will avoid the integration nightmare, at least initially.

Tradeoffs with Databases

Understanding the tradeoffs and wise choices involving databases and blockchains is a key competency that needs to be perfected. It starts with a clear understanding of the strengths and weaknesses of each approach (see Chapters 1 and 2).

Finding the right balance between what a blockchain is particularly good at, and marrying the derived benefits with back-end databases or existing applications is part of the magic that you need to continuously seek out. We are still learning what these boundaries are, and like the pendulum, we might swing excessively toward one side, then to another before finding a middleground.

Along with that topic is the issue of storing blockchain data for transactional, historical, analytical, and compliance reporting requirements.

Privacy

In a public blockchain, the default mode for any transaction's visibility is openness and transparency. This means that anyone can trace the path of a transaction including the value it holds, and its originating and destination address. That level of transparency was a non-starter in private blockchain implementations. However, it is now possible to achieve confidentiality in transactions by encrypting the values, and it is also possible to hide the identities via zero-knowledge proof schemes.

Security

The issue of blockchain security will be an everlasting one. We are still getting used to transaction finality by consensus (no matter what the form of consensus is), instead of a "database commit" which is a more deterministic method.

Large organizations, especially banks, have not been particularly interested in adopting public blockchains for their internal needs, citing potential security issues. The technical argument against the full security of public blockchains can easily be made the minute you introduce a shadow of a doubt on a potential scenario that might wreak havoc with the finality of a transaction. That alone is enough fear to form a deterring factor for staying away from blockchain blockchains, although the argument could be made in favor of their security.

Lack of Standards

There is an old adage: *the good thing about standards is there are so many of them to choose from*. In its early days, blockchain technology suffers from the opposite problem.

Standards arrive in two ways, typically. They either become *de facto* standards by virtue of market adoption, or they are developed and agreed upon *a priori*, by a standards committee, or a consortium group.

Standards bring with them a number of benefits, including some network effects, easier interoperability, shared implementation knowledge, potential lower costs, and less overall risk. Standards can tackle different layers, targeting technical, platform or process-related areas.

But here is a warning on standards. You do not generally compete on standards. They tend to level the playing field, and allow companies to compete on their own terms through the way in which they implement these standards. Your competitive edge might come from the speed of your implementation, or your ability to innovate beyond these standards. The blockchain will present the same opportunities and caveats for standards use. Standards will be necessary, but not sufficient.

MARKET/BUSINESS CHALLENGES

Some of the market and business challenges are macro-related, while others are more organization-specific.

Moving assets to the blockchain

The blockchain is a super fast rail that moves digital assets. But, the first challenge relates to placing the train on the rails before it can start moving swiftly. You can either create new assets directly on the blockchain, or move existing ones to it. Each approach introduces different considerations, although it may be easier to start by creating native assets, because you do not have to worry about full integration with your existing systems until later on.

Quality of Project Ideas

First experiences count, but if your initial entry points do not seem to provide a visible return, maybe the quality and ambition level of these projects are at fault. If the projects are timid, so will be the returns.

Critical Mass of Users

This applies to both consumer and business-to-business markets. Many consumer applications require hundreds of thousands, if not millions of users to be considered successful. On the business-to-business side, you need to get all members of a value chain aligned and involved along a given blockchain before they can start to reap commensurate value, and it takes time to accomplish these types of commitments.

Quality of Startups

Blockchain startups are not different from tech startups. They will come in all types of quality variety, and only a few of them break out into successfully viable businesses. Having many startups is a sign of ecosystem vibrancy, even if 90–95% of them do not succeed. Even failed startups produce experienced entrepreneurs who are more seasoned as a result of their work, and it makes them better at their craft the next time around. We should celebrate the availability of startups, regardless of the initial quality factor of every new venture.

Venture Capital

The availability of venture capital is essential for funding the incubation, production, and acceleration of innovation around the application of blockchain technology. Professional venture capitalists are well versed in funding risk and supporting entrepreneurs to help them realize their goals. We should expect a gradual increase in venture funding that flows into blockchain startups, and that would be a healthy sign.

In addition to venture capital, crowdfunding by self-issuing cryptocurrency or crypto-tokens is also another funding option. This approach carries some risks and uncertainty, due to lower external accountability controls. Although viable for certain cases, the success rates are not better than venture capital-funded startups.

Volatility of Cryptocurrency

Cryptocurrency volatility is a usage and confidence deterrent, but it is expected that volatility will gradually stabilize, tracking the increasing maturity and market adoption of the underlying technology behind each cryptocurrency. Eventually, bad actors and speculators will progressively become an insignificant minority with little to no impact on the overall health of cryptocurrencies.

Onboarding New Users

Most users cannot handle increased usage complexity, especially when the underlying technology is complex (the blockchain). Early blockchain applications may not have the best user experiences, but eventually, a user may not even know there is a blockchain behind their usage.

Few Poster Applications Companies

Where are the Amazons and eBays of the blockchain? Those kinds of companies become reference points and archetype models because they are the first proof points that you can build a viable business on the blockchain. We will need to witness the emergence of such companies, and see their success materialize through market adoption.

Not Enough Qualified Individuals Within Companies

It takes a while to convert thousands of employees to become experienced blockchain advocates. A critical mass of internal supporters and experts is also required inside organizations, so they can fuel a variety of blockchain experiments and create solutions themselves, without permission, just as Web applications and ideas have finally become second nature to most enterprises.

Costs Issues
It is not expensive to start dabbling with blockchain technology because much of it is free via open source licensing. However, full implementation will bear additional costs, not unlike the costs of typical information technology-related projects and deployments. Some Chief Information Officers (CIOs) may be reluctant to add to their tight budgets, until early returns on investment have been demonstrated.

Innovators Dilemma
It is difficult to innovate within your business model, because you will typically attempt to tie everything back to it, resulting in a shortsighted and limited view of what is possible. This is especially true if your business has a trust-related function (such as a clearing-house). Current intermediaries will encounter the hardest change, because the blockchain hits at the core of their value proposition. They will need to be creative, and dare disrupting themselves while folding some blockchain capabilities under their offerings, and creatively developing new value proposition elements. They will need to realize that it is better to shoot yourself in the foot, rather than to have someone else shoot you in the head. This will not be an easy transition, because changing business models could be difficult to achieve in large organizations for a variety of factors.

LEGAL/REGULATORY BARRIERS
Generally speaking, regulators and policy makers react in three different ways when faced with new technology:

1. Do nothing, and let the market mature and evolve on its own.
2. Control the choke points. For example, these choke points might be the cryptocurrency exchanges or software providers who will be required to get licensed.
3. Insert automatic regulation at the point of transaction, or somewhere during its journey. This might involve making room for the availability of direct data reporting via a backdoor, an information exhaust pipe, or a direct deduction on a transaction.

Unclear Regulations

As long as the position of regulators is not clarified, confusion and uncertainty will continue to exist for everyone involved in the blockchain space. The blockchain is a blockbuster technology that affects so many areas, and it is likely that different flavors of regulation will come at it from a variety of directions. This might add to the confusion. Just as the Internet was left alone to blossom in its earlier years, it would be advisable that blockchain technology is left alone until it matures further.

Regulation will eventually come to blockchains, but better late than early. A fundamental paradigm shift that regulators will need to come to grips with is that trust is now more open, and "free from central controls" who they typically regulated. The nature of trust is changing, but regulators are used to regulating the "trust providers." Will they learn to adjust when the trust provider is a blockchain, or a new type of intermediary that didn't fit the previous model of central choke point regulation? Specifically, the blockchain is decentralized by default, so it's more difficult to regulate decentralized entities than central ones. Therefore, we will need to see innovation in regulations. Maybe blockchains can get certified for example.

It is noteworthy that we are still regulating some aspects of cars more than one hundred years after they were invented, for example, by requiring lights to be turned on during the day, mandating seat belts, or limiting carbon dioxide emission levels. These regulations were certainly not part of the initial years of the automobile industry, but they were thought of after years of observation and experience. Imagine if regulators demanded automatic daylight sensors or inflatable air bags in 1910, two years following the Ford Model T introduction. Not only were these needs not thought of; even the basic technology behind these capabilities wasn't yet invented. The lesson here is that we do not really know what we need to regulate when a new technology is in its infancy of adoption.

Government Interferences

Targeting Bitcoin primarily, several governments did not feel comfortable with a currency that was not backed by a sovereign country's institutions. Some countries and central banks issued official warnings against Bitcoin usage during its early years, including Russia, China, and the European Union. Blockchains are not Bitcoin, yet they allow the creation and distribution of cryptocurrency, as well as assets with real value. The operations of blockchains will continue to be the subject of government scrutiny until politicians and policy makers feel more comfortable with their usage.

Governments can send the wrong signals to the market, to policy makers, and to law enforcement agencies, who are typically proxies to them. In addition, heavy-handed government actions risk short-circuiting the private sector leadership in blockchain technology, which is known to bear the fruit of innovation. Of course, government regulation may be applicable for consumer protection and certain other level of standards, but early interference will generally not be helpful.

Compliance Requirements

Compliance is an important activity, especially for financial services providers who spend billions of dollars annually, in order to stay up to the date on the latest laws and regulations.

Compliance and non-compliance are both costly, amounting to overhead that eats into profit margins. Some areas where compliance could offer breakthroughs might include:

- Accepting cryptocurrency-backed tokens as real value.
- Recognizing the finality of transactions that have passed through a blockchain.
- Allowing the necessary legal linkages to smart contracts.
- Permitting peer-to-peer counterparty validations via the blockchain.

Hype

It is difficult to characterize or agree on what constitutes hype or not. Sometimes the perception of hype is as damaging as hype itself. Excessive periods of hype are detrimental to the propagation of new technology, although markets almost always overshoot with hype expectations before pulling back into reality, and then they proceed accordingly. A most common form of hype typically comes from technology providers who are overzealous in their marketing approaches.

Taxation and Reporting

Early blockchain platforms were focused on transactions, and not reporting. However, these platforms will need better taxation and reporting capabilities so that their output can be fed into traditional accounting systems. There will be solutions that address this sector.

BEHAVIORAL/EDUCATIONAL CHALLENGES

Lack of Understanding of Potential Value

A lack of a comprehensive understanding of the basic capabilities surrounding the blockchain will deter any smart executive from seeing the fullness of its potential value. This challenge will be only solved via a concerted effort to get educated about the blockchain and its potential. This was my impetus for my writing *The Business Blockchain.*

Limited Executive Vision

Some executives will just see what they want to see, either because they have not spent enough time to fully study the blockchain, or perhaps they are afraid of learning it to avoid handling the disruption potential on their business. It does take some time to fully wrap your mind around the many possibilities of the blockchain. Executives with a fear of the blockchain will dial down their vision to fit their own reality, which is typically painted in restrictive colors.

Change management

The blockchain is about business process reengineering—at least, if you want to reap more fundamental benefits. Quick or easy projects may not have the depth of required change that is needed to yield more gains. Change is hard to accomplish in large organizations.

Trusting a Network

Blockchain skeptics might think: we already trust one another, and we have century old institutions that perform that kind of trust, so why do we need to put trust inside a network?

Trusting a network of computers that perform mathematical computations instead of a "known, trusted" party that you can see requires a new mental paradigm that we are not used to. Eventually, we will come to grips with the fact that the *trust is in the network*—and it is a new form of trust. Let us remember that Internet payments were not completely trusted during the early Web years (1994–1998), at least not by the banks. We had to go through special "payment gateways" that were set-up specifically to perform that trust function while dissociating them from the banking systems who didn't want to touch untrusted technology. Soon enough, paying on the Web with a credit card became wildly accepted, and most current Web users will probably not remember these early days of trepidation and fear, although the similarity with trusting blockchains is strikingly familiar.

As much as we will initially fret over the availability of block-chains as trust services delivery networks, they will be eventually be taken for granted, just as Internet access is taken for granted today in most parts of the world.

Few Best Practices

Given the scarcity of Blockchain implementation experiences, the real best practices are few and far between. Following the initial fury towards the discovery of use cases, sharing best practices and benchmarking will be the next popular activity.

Low Usability Factor

Bitcoin's original usability was not so great, as reflected by the dozens of software wallet applications that sprung out since 2010. Web-based hosted cryptocurrency exchanges provided an easier user interface, via an online banking-like familiar look and feel. Although the latter were criticized for a lack of decentralization, they did offer a desirable ease of use that spurred user adoption.

The next generation of blockchain-based applications will come in two flavors: either they will be decentralized applications (like OpenBazaar), or they will look like regular Web applications with back-end decentralization. In either case, their usability will be intricately tied to the specific function they are addressing. For example, it will be a financial trade application, or a land registration application, and the blockchain will do its work without being overly visible to the user, except in allowing them to reap the benefits they bring.

KEY IDEAS FROM CHAPTER THREE

1. The list of challenges facing the blockchain is long, but there is not a lot of difference with the Internet's situation, back in 1997, when we knocked down all these barriers one by one, while some of them went away on their own.

2. There are technical, business/market, legal/regulatory, and behavioral/educational challenges to the blockchain's evolution.

3. Some of the most important challenges include scalability (technical), innovation (business), trusting a network (behavioral), and modern regulation (legal).

4. Just as we continued to scale the Internet 30 years after its invention, we will continue to solve and update the blockchain's scalability needs.

5. Just as we continued to update automobile safety regulations in ways that were unforeseen during the invention moment, we will continue to update the regulatory requirements around the blockchain over the lifetime of its evolution.

NOTES

1. A term popularized in Clayton Christensen's book (*The Innovator's Dilemma*) suggesting that successful companies can put too much emphasis on customers' current needs, and fail to adopt new technology or business models, https://en.wikipedia.org/wiki/The_Innovator%27s_Dilemma. List of U.S. executive branch czars, https://en.wikipedia.org/wiki/List_of_U.S._executive_branch_czars.

2. Source: Author's sample survey of market leaders, April 2016.

3. Java, https://en.wikipedia.org/wiki/Java_%28programming_language%29.

4. IDC Study, http://www.infoq.com/news/2014/01/IDC-software-developers.

5. These are popular programming languages.

6. https://cryptoconsortium.org/

□–□–4–□–□

BLOCKCHAIN IN FINANCIAL SERVICES

"The worst place to develop a new business model is from within your existing business model."

—CLAYTON CHRISTENSEN

FINANCIAL SERVICES INSTITUTIONS will be challenged by how much they are willing to bend their business models to accommodate the weight of the blockchain. Their default position will be to only slightly open the door, expecting to let as many benefits seep in, with the least amount of opening. The challengers (mostly startups) will try to kick that door open as much as possible, expecting to throw the incumbents off balance.

Much of the blockchain's technological innovation in financial services is driven by startups. But financial institutions, like any other industry, can innovate by applying that technology. Startups are like a strange beast when it comes to how banks view them. They will first get examined and kept at close proximity, but benefits do not happen via symbiosis. In reality, large organizations are degrees removed from most startups. Their initial interest is like visiting animals in the zoo. The litmus test is to bring the technology home to see if it will survive domestication.

Any large organization will be challenged when facing large amounts of external innovation that surpasses their internal abilities to absorb it or usurp it.

Industry activities are coming from two different directions. On one hand, startups and technology products and services companies are entering the market. On the other hand, organizations will start to study the market and generate a long list of use cases and target areas. The challenge will be to match the right technical and business approaches to the chosen use cases, projects and initiatives.

Banks will be required to get their hands dirty and learn the new technologies directly. They will also need to get their minds dirty and try ideas even if they risk failing. The more basic experience they acquire early on, the faster they will be able to progress from their initial work to more ground-breaking undertakings.

This chapter does not prescribe specific solutions to specific organizations. Rather, it lays out how financial services organizations can think about the blockchain. How to think about the blockchain is useful, because it allows you to uncover your own strategies. After all, you know your business better than anyone else.

ATTACKED BY THE INTERNET AND FINTECH

To understand how the blockchain will affect financial services institutions, we must go back to their recent history with the Internet, and also look at the advent of FinTech companies that offered competing services by embracing a technology-forward product approach.

Banks have been relying on information technology (IT) since the early introduction of the mainframe computers in the late 1950s, but the term FinTech only became popular around 2013. It is ironic that technology has always played a key role in a bank's operations, yet one could argue that banks did not innovate much with the Internet. Traditionally, the IT focus at banks was oriented towards running back-end operations (including clients' accounts and transactions), supporting branch retail functions, linking automated teller machines, processing payments from point-of-sale retail gateways, being globally interconnected with their partners or inter-banking networks, and delivering a variety of financial products ranging from simple loans to sophisticated trading instruments.

In 1994, the Web arrived, and with it the potential to offer an alternative front-end entry point for any service. However, most banks pushed back on that innovation window, because they were entrenched in delivering services inside their retail branches, or via one-on-one business relationships. They did not see the Web as a catalyst for bigger change, so they adapted the Internet at their own pace, and according to their own limited assumptions. Fast forward to 2016, more than 20 years into the Web's commercialization, and one could argue that banks only gave their customers Internet banking (with mobile access later), online brokerage, and online bill payments. The reality is that customers are not going to the branch as often (or at all), and they are not licking as many stamps to pay their bills. Meanwhile, FinTech growth is happening; it was a total response to banks' lack of radical innovation.

PayPal was the quintessential payment disruptor. Thousands of FinTech companies followed their lead and started offering alternative financial services solutions. With 179 million active users and $282 billiion total payments volume by the end of 2015, PayPal was "a truly global platform that is available in more than 200 markets, allowing customers to get paid in more than 100 currencies, withdraw funds from their bank accounts in 57 currencies and hold balances in their PayPal accounts in 26 currencies."[1]

PayPal has direct relationships with hundreds of local banks around the world, making them arguably the only global financial services provider that virtually knows no boundaries. PayPal's success had fundamental implications: it demonstrated that alternative financial services companies could be viable, just by building bridges and ramps into incumbent banking institutions. As a side note, in 2014, ApplePay took a page from PayPal, and inserted itself once again between the banks and their customers by hijacking the point-of-sale moments via multipurpose smartphones. If you talk to any banker in the world, they will admit that ApplePay and PayPal are vexing examples of competition that simply eats into their margins, and they could not prevent their onslaught.

By 2015, more than $19 billion in venture funding had been poured into FinTech startups.[2] Many of them were focused on just a few popular areas: loans, wealth management, and payments. Some startups have gone as far as offering full banking services via mobile-only, an approach that is appealing to millennials. This proves that a new form of bank can be created from scratch, without legacy baggage.

What is interesting is that FinTech startups didn't initially attack incumbents head-on, knowing it is risky and costly. Rather, their entry points were in adjacent, uncontested, neglected, or underserved territories; they appear at first to be avoiding the incumbents. Startups begin small and look harmless. They are ignored, until they suddenly become significant and unstoppable.

This backdrop is important. Blockchain may follow the same trajectory as FinTech thus far, turning footholds into significant beachheads or fully-fledged businesses. Some blockchain-based startups are already slowly attacking pain points within the financial services market, offering solutions to existing players, while others are following a cooperative process to fertilize flavors of shared infrastructure or services solutions. Other startups are dreaming the impossible by ignoring incumbents, and offering new solutions to a virgin market.

Those who do not learn from history are condemned to repeat it. If banks do not adapt more radically than they did with the

Internet, they will suffer the consequences. If FinTech was about challenging banks' payments systems, blockchain promises to not only continue to unbundle the banks, but seems intent on disrupting a whole gamut of traditional inter-institutional processes, from cross border to clearinghouses.

For financial institutions, the future of blockchain technologies will begin via two parallel paths. It is a story of good and bad news. On the bad news side, some of the blockchain startups will be going after their business, FinTech style. But the good news is that blockchain technology is perfect for streamlining much of banking operations.

If you are an optimist, there is a third outcome. Banks and the entire financial services industry might decide to seriously reinvent themselves. In that difficult to achieve scenario, there will be winners and losers, and parts of the overall segment would shrink—but it might emerge stronger in the long term.

Blockchains will not signal the end of banks, but innovation must permeate faster than the Internet did in 1995–2000. The early blockchain years are formative and important because they are training grounds for this new technology, and whoever has trained well will win. The strong will not die. Banks should not only see the blockchain as a cost savings lever. It is very much about finding new opportunities that can grow their top line.

WHY CAN'T THERE BE A GLOBAL BANK?

To a skeptic, it sounds like a rhetorical question, given that Bitcoin was destined to become the underpinning nerve for a new type of global financial system that is borderless. Bitcoin's vision is a globally decentralized money network with users at the edges of it.

We should ask the question—since Bitcoin is global and universal, why is not there a truly global Bitcoin bank?

This is a tricky question, because Bitcoin's philosophy is about decentralization, whereas a bank is everything about centrally managed relationships. However, a global bank with no restrictions on borders or transactions would be interesting to users that want to conduct global transactions wherever they are in the world with the same ease as using a credit card.

But here's the sad news: this fictitious global bank will never exist, because local regulatory hurdles are too high and too real. No existing startup or bank has the incentive or desire to become that "ultra" bank. The hurdles that Uber (the ride sharing service) has faced against the global taxi cartels would pale in comparison to the complexities and intricacies of the regulatory, compliance, and legal barriers that are intrinsic to each local financial services system around the world.

Do you know why HSBC is not really the world's leading global bank, despite being in 72 countries? Do you know why Coinbase is not really the "world's" leading Bitcoin exchange, despite being the largest and only exchange available in 27 countries?

There is a common answer to these two questions: regulatory restrictions. This means that your account's capabilities are confined to the country you belong to, just like a traditional bank account. As a user, you do not really get the feeling of being global. HSBC and Coinbase may be global companies, but their customers do not have borderless services privileges.

Luckily, within a pure Bitcoin world, that potential global bank is *you*, if you are armed with a cryptocurrency wallet. A local cryptocurrency wallet skirts some of the legalities that existing banks and bank look-alikes (cryptocurrency exchanges) need to adhere to, but without breaking any laws. You take "your bank" with you wherever you travel, and as long as that wallet has local onramps and bridges into the non-cryptocurrency terrestrial world, then you have a version of a global bank in your pocket.

This backdrop about the evolution of consumer-based cryptocurrency trading is important, because it demonstrates that we can achieve another form of connectedness by virtue of the blockchain itself, achieving a SWIFT-like[3] effect. The 50 or so cryptocurrency exchanges that exist in various parts of the world are not overtly linked together, yet they are seamlessly connected by the blockchain. This is a significant confirmation that a blockchain is a global network that knows no boundaries. As much as banks disdain Bitcoin and its blockchain, they should see these capabilities as a demonstration of what is possible if you let a blockchain become a global network.

One could argue that the cryptocurrency networks (enabled by blockchains) are going to be more important than the currency itself. New decentralized networks also allow the trading of any digital asset, financial instrument, or real world asset that is linked to a cryptocurrency-based token (a form of proxy attachment to a blockchain). Whether using a standalone wallet, or a brokerage type of account, users already have access to various familiar actions that we typically conduct with money: buy, sell, pay, get paid, transfer, save, or borrow. Incidentally, PayPal offers the same functions.

Maybe one day, we could each become our own virtual bank. Advanced cryptocurrency wallets could become to the world of crypto-finance networks what the browser was to the World Wide Web, and be these new entry points for monetary transactions. Hopefully, regulators can evolve with the technology without a heavy-handed approach, as long as users are not bad actors, pay their taxes, and do not conduct illegal activities.

Getting to a global bank status is not easy. There is a historical reminder that online banking is not enough to produce a global bank. Several attempts were made, from 1995–2000, to form Internet-only banks,[4] starting with Security First Network Bank (SFNB), the world's first Internet bank, but each attempt was confined to the jurisdiction they were created in. SFNB, CompuBank, Net.B@nk, Netbank AG, Wingspan, E-LOAN, Bank One, VirtualBank and others are examples, but they did not survive the dot-com crash of 2000.

The new crop of online/mobile only banks and financial services startups such as Atom, Tandem, Mondo, ZenBanx, GoBank, Moven, and Number26, do offer a new generation of services that challenges traditional banks. But if any of these services aims to become global, they still need to knock down the local financial regulatory barriers.

If you were a millennial today, you would not think twice about not using a traditional bank because most of the services you are attracted to are offered by alternative financial services companies, primarily due to these innovative FinTech startups that sprung up in the past decade. A typical "millennial financial stack" includes an array of new FinTech services, and only the most innovative products from a traditional bank.[5]

Typically, we use traditional banking networks to transfer any type of money. I can see a future where we are using a blockchain infrastructure to transfer any money, including cryptocurrency and sovereign currency. This means that traditional money may be coming to cryptocurrency wallets and exchange brokerage accounts faster than cryptocurrency being accepted inside traditional online banking accounts.

BANKS AS BACKENDS

One likely future scenario is for banks to function as backends, or a lateral window, as we will be transacting and moving money externally via our smartphones, apps, cryptocurrency accounts, or Web services directly. Although a truly global bank or exchange may not happen any time soon, the feelings and behaviors of a global bank are needed.

In this scheme, banks become financial on-ramps and off-ramps, but they will not be centers of your wallet.

The more we link our bank accounts to external services and applications, the more we realize that we are living in a world of decentralized banking. The trend has started, and it is more than anecdotal because it is happening frequently and with increasing impact.

Here are some examples:

- If you run a ticketed event and collect fees from attendees, you can link that event's payment process to your bank account and get paid quickly. For example, this is accomplished by linking Eventbrite via PayPal (as the payment processor) to your account.

- If your cryptocurrency exchange account is connected to your bank account, you could move money around the world in less than 10 minutes at the cost of pennies in fees, and then you (or the recipient) can transfer the money back and forth to a bank account. Most exchanges provide multiple ways to deposit or withdraw money, including wire transfers, drafts, money orders, Western Union, check, debit card, Visa, PayPal, or Virtual Visa, many of them for free. Some of these exchanges even offer foreign currency exchange services in real-time between a variety of cryptocurrencies and popular currencies, such the U.S. dollar, Canadian dollar, Euro, British pound, and Japanese yen. Already, these are more capabilities than what the average bank user can do without visiting a branch.

- If you are running a crowdfunding campaign (such as on Kickstarter), you are also required to link your bank account. At the completion of a successful campaign, your earnings are automatically deposited into that account.

- When you link your ApplePay account to checkout and pay for items in seconds, the money is actually coming directly from one of your bank or credit card accounts.

- When you take an Uber ride, Uber makes a pull request to charge your credit card, automatically.

- A Venmo account that lets you receive money instantly from a friend, also lets you push that balance back to your bank account (or vice-versa).

These examples are few but significant. The point and reality of all these situations is that we, as consumers, are doing more interesting things with these new ancillary services than we can directly from our bank accounts. More importantly, the banks alone would not allow us to accomplish what these linkages enable, which is why we have to go through these new intermediaries. These new services are liberating us from the restrictive features of a traditional bank account.

Retail merchants have had a taste of this two-tier separation for a while, via their point-of-sale terminals that take money from customers and see it automatically deposited in their bank accounts. That was their version of linked services, but now this is more widely expanded to consumers.

Concurrently, the pendulum is swinging between local and global linkages. Traditionally, banks have had strong local anchors because that's how they were started. Later, they built global linkages between them at great expense and effort, through networks that are proprietary and relatively expensive to maintain. But with the advent of Bitcoin and blockchains as global rails, we already have powerful global networks that are seamless across boundaries, and we are now complementing the reach of those new networks by adding local anchors and local users, via your bank account. Suddenly, your traditional bank account will ressemble nothing more than a node on the global cloud of financial networks.

Strongly operating locally has killed the banks' abilities to join the more open global Web of financial services—except through on-ramps and off-ramps—and no longer function as the main money highway. Banks risk being on the outside looking in, if they continue allowing more on-ramps and exits to the new world of cryptocurrencies. Otherwise, they will become islands themselves.

Although regulation has offered consumers some personal protection benefits, the natural regulatory reactions are to continue erecting higher barriers for local entry (for competitive reasons), resulting in pushing users to more global and seamless services because the game is now happening via the web's interstitials.

The decentralization of banking is here. It just has not been evenly distributed yet.

BLOCKCHAIN INSIDE REGULATIONS VERSUS PERMISSIONLESS INNOVATION

The distinction between permissionless blockchains (ones that are public and open for anyone's participation), and permissioned blockchains (ones that operate in private settings, via an invitation-only model) is correlated to the degree of innovation that follows.

The default state and starting position for innovation is to be permissionless. Consequently, permissioned and private blockchain implementations will have a muted innovation potential. At least in the true sense of the word, not for technical reasons, but for regulatory ones, because these two aspects are tied together.

We are seeing the first such case unfold within the financial services sector, that seems to be embracing the blockchain fully; but they are embracing it according to their own interpretation of it, which is to make it live within the regulatory constraints they have to live with. What they are really talking about is "applying innovation," and not creating it. So, the end-result will be a dialed-down version of innovation.

That is a fact, and I am calling this situation the "Being Regulated Dilemma," a pun on the innovator's dilemma. Like the innovator's dilemma, regulated companies have a tough time extricating themselves from the current regulations they have to operate within. So, when they see technology, all they can do is to implement it within the satisfaction zones of regulators. Despite the blockchain's revolutionary prognosis, the banks cannot outdo themselves, so they risk only guiding the blockchain to live within their constrained, regulated world.

INNOVATION POTENTIAL FOR THE BLOCKCHAIN

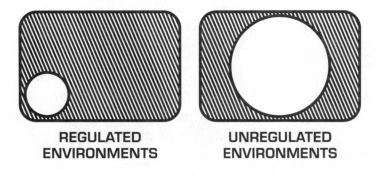

REGULATED ENVIRONMENTS

UNREGULATED ENVIRONMENTS

It is a lot easier to start innovating outside the regulatory boxes, both figuratively and explicitly. Few banks will do this because it is more difficult.

Simon Taylor, head of the blockchain innovation group at Barclays, sums it up: "I do not disagree the best use cases will be outside regulated financial services. Much like the best users of cloud and big data are not the incumbent blue chip organizations. Still their curiosity is valuable for funding and driving forward the entire space." I strongly agree; there is hope some banks will contribute to the innovation potential of the blockchain in significant ways as they mature their understanding and experiences with this new technology.

An ending note to banks is that radical innovation can be a competitive advantage, but only if it is seen that way. Otherwise, innovation will be dialed down to fit their own reality, which is typically painted in restrictive colors.

It would be useful to see banks succeed with the blockchain, but they need to push themselves further in terms of understanding what the blockchain can do. They need to figure out how they will serve their customers better, and not just how they will serve themselves better. Banks should innovate more by dreaming up use cases that we have not thought about yet, preferably in the non-obvious category.

LANDSCAPE OF BLOCKCHAIN COMPANIES IN FINANCIAL SERVICES

At the end of 2015, I published a detailed landscape of blockchain companies in financial services,[6] and tallied 268 entries, across 27 categories. I followed it with an analysis of the sector by releasing another popular slide deck[7] that gathered 175,000 views on Slideshare within a month of being published.

The landscape of blockchain companies that are targeting financial services can be divided across three sectors:

- Infrastructure and Base Protocols
- Middleware and Services
- Applications and Solutions

The following table details the various players, and the market forces at play.

APPLICATIONS AND SOLUTIONS	
• Brokerage services	• Trading platforms
• Cryptocurrency exchanges	• Brokerage services
• Software wallets	• Payroll
• Hardware wallets	• Insurance
• Merchant and retail services	• Investments
• Financial data providers	• Loans
• Trade finance solutions	• Global/Local money services
• Compliance and identity	• Capital markets solutions
• Payments integrations	• Teller machines

MIDDLEWARE & SERVICES	
• Technology services providers	• General purpose APIs
• Blockchain platforms	• Special purpose APIs
• Software development environments	• Smart contracts tools

INFRASTRUCTURE & BASE PROTOCOLS	
• Public consensus blockchains	• Microtransactions infrastructure
• Private consensus blockchains	• Miners

BLOCKCHAIN APPLICATIONS IN FINANCIAL SERVICES

From an internal implementation point of view, the blockchain's evolution in Financial Services will happen according to a progressive segmentation of major applications areas:

- Consumer facing products
- B2B services
- Trading and capital markets
- Back-end processes
- Inter-industry intermediary services

The following diagram illustrates how these categories might unfold along an increasingly complex timeframe of implementation.

BLOCKCHAIN IN FINANCIAL SERVICES

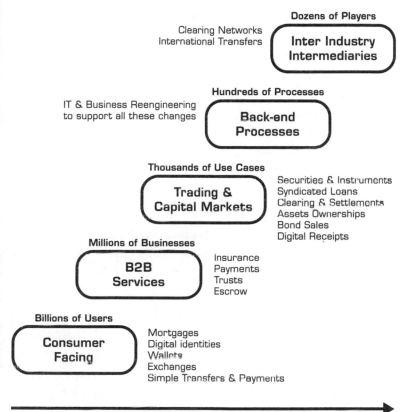

It is worth highlighting some practical approaches that are beginning to emerge, and are pointing towards the future:

- In November 2015, ConsenSys demonstrated a two-party Total Return Swap financial contract that made use of underlying identity, reputation, and general ledger components, and ran on the Microsoft Azure cloud platform.

- In February 2016, Clearmatics announced it was developing a new clearing platform for over-the-counter derivatives that it calls a Decentralized Clearing Network (DCN). It allows a consortium of clearing members to automate contract valuation, margining, trade compression, and close-out without a central clearing counterparty (CCP), or third-party intermediation.[8]

- In March 2016, forty of the world's largest banks demonstrated a test system for trading fixed income, using five different blockchain technologies (as part of the R3 CEV consortium).

- In March 2016, Cambridge Blockchain designed a catastrophe bond transaction process that included counterparty validation on the blockchain, and an automated workflow enabling users to maintain privacy while selectively revealing limited attributes of their identities required for pre-trade authentication and compliance.

What is common to each of the above cases, is that these transactions were done from start to finish on a peer-to-peer basis, without central intermediaries or clearinghouses in the middle. The counterparties did not need to know each other or require a third-party to intermediate the transaction. Decentralization and peer-to-peer transaction finality are key blockchain innovations that must be preserved in order to maximize the potential impact of blockchain implementations. Generically, the counterparties' identities and reputations are automatically verified on the blockchain via wallet addresses or built-in AML/KYC (Anti-Money Laundering / Know Your Customer) attestations or collateral requirements. Then, the transaction terms are entered into a smart contract and published on the blockchain, while simultaneously storing the associated regulatory agreement (for example, an International Swaps and Derivatives Association (ISDA) Master Agreement) on a decentralized peer-to-peer file distribution protocol (for example on the InterPlanetary File System). The last reporting step could be entered into a standard database performing compliance requirements, although the degree of P2P purity would be diminished if centralized databases are used.

There are many applications where a blockchain or distributed consensus ledger solution will make sense. At the risk of not naming all of them, here are the largest segments that will be affected:

- Bonds
- Swaps
- Derivatives
- Commodities
- Unregistered/Registered securities
- Over-the-counter markets
- Collateral management
- Syndicated loans
- Warehouse receipts
- Repurchase market

STRATEGIC QUESTIONS FOR FINANCIAL SERVICES

Theme 1: Blockchains Touch the Core of Banking, Can They React?

In Chapter 2, we introduced the word *ATOMIC* as a way to remember the programmability aspect of blockchains along six interrelated areas: *Assets, Trust, Ownership, Money, Identity, and Contracts*. Add to these concepts the fact the blockchain is about *decentralization, disintermediation, and distributed ledgers*, and you quickly realize that these subjects are very much part of the core of banking. When a single technology touches almost every core part of your business model, you need to pay attention, as it will be a challenging encounter. Banks will be required to apply rigorous thinking to flush out their plans and positions vis-à-vis each one of these major blockchain parameters. They cannot ignore what happens when their core is being threatened.

Theme 2: Follow, Lead, or Leapfrog

Financial services institutions can follow three strategic directions. It is proposed they choose all three directions.

1. *Follow.* By participating in consortia, standards groups, or open source projects, financial institutions can reap the benefits of a collaborative approach to figure out where the blockchain can contribute. Some of these efforts might lead to lubricating inter-banking relationships, while others will expose members to usable technology and best practices that can be imported inside the organization.

2. *Lead.* This pertains to leading a number of initiatives internally where you discover and implement where the blockchain can streamline various parts of your business. This is where internal capabilities need to be proactively built, either internally or with the help of external services providers.

3. *Leapfrog*. This might be the most difficult phase to initiate, because it will focus on thinking outside of your business model boundaries and inside new innovation territory. There is a key outcome-related distinction between this direction and the previous ones: leapfrogging should generate new revenues in new areas (top line growth), whereas the two will more likely be oriented towards saving costs or streamlining operations.

Theme 3: Regulations, Regulations, & Regulations

The variety of financial services regulatory authorities around the world rivals the number of ice cream flavor varieties. More than 200 regulatory bodies exist in 150 countries, and many of them have been eyeing the blockchain and pondering regulatory updates pertaining to it.

Imagine if each one of these bodies issued their own type of blockchain regulations, without coordination, or without due consideration for the full implications of such policies. Not only would a mess ensue, but potentially the blockchain technology industry might get killed as a result of the resulting massive confusion.

The Commissioner of the U.S. Commodity Futures Trading Commission (CFTC), J. Christopher Giancarlo, underscored that specific point during a speech he made in March 2016 at a conference organized by The Depository Trust & Clearing Corporation (DTCC). He said:

"Yet, this investment faces the danger that when regulation does come, it will come from a dozen different directions with different restrictions stifling crucial technological development before it reaches fruition."

When the Internet arrived, governments and policy makers were smart enough to not regulate it too early, and that contributed to its growth. The reality facing financial services institutions is, once again, they will be at the mercy of the regulators when it comes to the blockchain.

Banks are between a rock and a hard place: the blockchain is global, but regulations have forced them to focus on serving local needs. Regulation has protected them but it could also hurt them at the same time (if it does not evolve).

Theme 4: Legalizing Blockchain Transactions

At the heart of reaching widespread adoption for blockchain-based business interactions, transactions that are processed by a blockchain will need to be recognized as legally binding and acceptable within compliance requirements. This might involve revisiting recordkeeping or compliance rules, or at least ensuring that new regulation does not specifically prevent institutions from using the blockchain to run these transactions, or at least to allowing them to experiment with that technology to continue showcasing new capabilities, and learn where it can lead.

A skeptical question might be: If trust is the key blockchain enabler, banks already trust one another, so why do we need a "trust network"? The answer lies in the fact that when we examine the cost of running the current trust system, we will find these costs have become excessive. This is in part due to regulations, and in part due to the required complex integrations between the proprietary systems of each financial services institution. Add to that the indirect losses resulting from delays in settlement closures, and you endup with a high cost margin that is ripe for the shaving.

Theme 5: Do Banks Want a Better Inter-Banking Network?

Each bank has their own proprietary systems, and they are required to use private networks they either own or control in order to move money that is in their possession. It is a known fact that regulations and multi-party intermediary steps are principal reasons why inter-banking settlements take days to clear.

By virtue of its powerful vision of a single ledger, the blockchain is questioning if banks can continue depending on proprietary systems that are silos to one another. The prospects of a more homogeneous, but also more openly traversable audit trail of global transactions could offer unique insights and lower risks. In a correspondence, Juan Llanos, a certified AML and risk expert in FinTech and cryptography told me:

"Today's AML paradigm is based on heavy customer due diligence and light (intra-company) transaction monitoring. Blockchain tech enables enhanced transactional analyses that were not possible before. In the pre-blockchain era, regulated financial institutions could only do intra-company transactional analysis, and had to share information via analog or documentary methods. Network-wide analytics that are possible with blockchains transcend industries and jurisdictional borders. There is now an opportunity to trade-off reduced KYC requirements (thus fomenting financial inclusion) for the increased behavioral transparency afforded by the blockchain."

The key question becomes whether law enforcement authorities and regulators are able to embrace this paradigm shift. In the long term, a large part of compliance could move towards intelligence, because blockchain networks offer more transparency and analytical oversight.

Theme 6: Can the Banks Redefine Themselves or Will They Just Improve a Little?

Here is a summary of the dilemma. Banks do not want to change banking. Startups want to change banking. Blockchain wants to change the world.

Banks will need to decide if they see the blockchain as a series of Band-Aids, or if they are willing to find the new patches of opportunity. That is why I have been advocating that they should embrace (or buy) the new cryptocurrency exchanges, not because these enable Bitcoin trades, but because they are a new generation of financial networks that has figured out how to transfer assets, financial instruments, or digital assets swiftly and reliably, in essence circumventing the network towers and expense bridges that the current financial services industry relies upon.

KEY IDEAS FROM CHAPTER FOUR

1. We would be asking a lot if we asked financial services institutions to fully embrace the blockchain. In reality, what they will do initially is to pick and choose what they like and disregard what they do not like about it.

2. Although a global bank or exchange is not happening any time soon, the feelings and behaviors of a global bank are needed. The blockchain can help.

3. The Financial Services sector will need to stall new regulation while simultaneously updating the existing regulation to accommodate the innovation introduced by the blockchain.

4. The litmus test is to run transactions without a central clearinghouse in the middle. Verifying identity and validating counterparties can be done in a peer-to-peer manner on the blockchain, and that is the preferred method that organizations should be trying to perfect.

5. Strategic decisions await financial institutions, and they must have the courage to leapfrog, and not just advance to the next level playing field and be content with it.

NOTES

1. PayPal "Who we are," https://www.paypal.com/webapps/mpp/about.

2. The Pulse of FinTech, 2015 in Review, KPMG and CB Insights, https://assets.kpmg.com/content/dam/kpmg/pdf/2016/03/the-pulse-of-fintech.pdf.

3. "The Society for Worldwide Interbank Financial Telecommunication (SWIFT) provides a network that enables financial institutions worldwide to send and receive information about financial transactions in a secure, standardized and reliable environment." (Source: Wikipedia) http://swift.com/.

4. "Virtual Rivals," *The Economist*, 2000, http://www.economist.com/node/348364.

5. "My Financial Stack as a Millennial," Sachin Rekhi, http://www.sachinrekhi.com/my-financial-stack-as-a-millennial.

6. Update to the Global Landscape of Blockchain Companies in Financial Services, William Mougayar, http://startupmanagement.org/2015/12/08/update-to-the-global-landscape-of-blockchain-companies-in-financial-services/.

7. "Blockchain 2015: Strategic Analysis in Financial Services," William Mougayar, http://www.slideshare.net/wmougayar/blockchain-2015-analyzing-the-blockchain-in-financial-services.

8. "Ethereum-inspired Clearmatics to save OTC markets from eternal darkness," Ian Allison, IB Times, http://www.ibtimes.co.uk/ethereum-inspired-clearmatics-save-otc-markets-eternal-darkness-1545180.

☐-☐-⑤-☐-☐

LIGHTHOUSE INDUSTRIES & NEW INTERMEDIARIES

"Fool you are to say you learn by your experience! I prefer to profit by others' mistakes, and avoid the price of my own."
—PRINCE OTTO VON BRISMARCK

THIS CHAPTER COVERS the blockchain's impact in a handful of industries outside of banking and capital markets.

Outside the realm of corporations, there are larger, global problems that are potential targets for the blockchain, and they are related to the economy, industries, government, or society. Some of these problems are rooted by philosophical or ideological underpinnings. Pick your flavor of grievance or issue around the world, and there might be a decentralization-based alternative flavor for a solution that is undoubtedly linked to a blockchain.

If you want to look at true innovation with the blockchain, the common denominator points to no incumbents in that equation. The new startups give no regards to existing central services, and they attempt to build a better service that takes advantage of the decentralization features of the blockchain.

Here is another new paradigm about the blockchain: data and programs are public. Semi-public to be precise, because the information is cryptographically secure, and only visible if you have access rights. It means anyone can publish data on the blockchain. Previously, everything important was behind hidden databases, or a physical service counter, and we had to go somewhere to verify something. Now, we will learn to expose data, and break databases into pieces, without security fears.

You need to believe that you can safely run programs on a public infrastructure that is arguably more secure than some traditional computing environments. Blockchain infrastructures have multiple built-in redundancies, and are very resilient.

THE NEW INTERMEDIARIES

Old intermediaries that are threatened by technology always die hard. They do not simply roll over. They keep fighting while they are shrinking. Newspapers, cable television providers, and travel agents are some examples.

The blockchain attacks some old intermediaries: central counterparty clearinghouses, notaries, escrow services, and any services with a built-in trust component. While the blockchain chips away at some functions from these existing intermediaries, it also enables the creation of new players.

Initially, blockchain services will look like "alternative" offerings that are adjunct to the mainstream, but this is how Internet services started. With increased adoption, these alternative choices become mainstream.

Unbundling is the main reason why new intermediaries emerge. Unbundling takes away some layers of functionality, creating entry point weaknesses for new intermediaries who exploit them. What is unbundled around the core stops protecting the core.

The Web was a new intermediary platform that replaced newspapers, entertainment media, and travel agents.

Who will be the new blockchain-based intermediaries?

Proof of Trust Authorities

Soon, we will be able to get a "proof for everything." The vision is this: trust checking should be a frictionless process, as easy as your searches on Google.

We can imagine a flurry of blockchain-based services that will become the new "trust authorities." You start by time-stamping something. Others can verify what you have done. Here are some examples to get inspired from:

- *Proof-of-Identity:* Get your identity verified by block-chain-based certificate authorities.
- *Proof-of-Existence:* Record an audio/video, take a picture or receive a file, and share these proofs.
- *Oracles-as-a-Business:* Oracles will become reference authorities, because they contain useful information that is always updated.
- *Smart Contracts-as-a-Service:* Consult smart contracts directories straight from your browser (e.g., Pax Directory)
- *Proof-of-Affidavit:* Verify that you purchased something, such as a licensed arm, a lotto ticket, a medication, or a fishing license.
- *Proof-of-Location:* Prove that you were in a given location.
- *Proof-of-Ownership:* Answer the question, who owns this?
- *Proof-of-Leads Generation:* Help ensure that you are buying credible marketing leads, without fraud.

The DAOs Are Coming

One representation of decentralized governance is depicted by the arrival of Distributed Autonomous Organizations (DAOs) whose governance and operations run on the blockchain. Arguably, this could be the epitome of business decentralization. In the near future, anyone will be able to "work" for a DAO without permission, and benefit economically from it.

The concept of a Distributed Autonomous Organization/ Corporation (DAO/DAC) is an idealistic outcome of the crypto-tech revolution. Its roots originate in themes on organizational decentralization that were depicted by Ori Brafman in *The Starfish and the Spider* (2007), and ones about "peer production," aptly described by Yochai Benkler in *The Wealth of Networks* (2007). But these two themes were recently joined by the advent of cryptocurrency-related technologies by Dan Larimer who observed that Bitcoin is the original DAC, and Vitalik Buterin who expanded on that construct by generalizing it further as a DAO, noting that the DAO has "internal capital." Deregulation of crowdfunding and unbundling of services were two additionally paired themes that added to this combustion, and the whole thing was turbo-charged by a crypto-tech governance layer of technologies and trust-based automations to allow DAOs to "run without any human involvement under the control of an incorruptible set of business rules."[1]

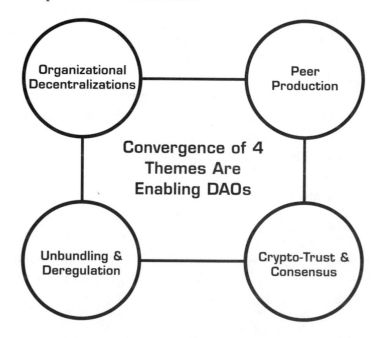

We are still missing real experiences and a deeper dive into the realities of operating a DAO. Certainly not all DAOs will be born by following a cookbook. And there will be variations and shades of purity in DAO principles, for practical purposes.

So how do you get there, and what are the pieces of the puzzle from an operational/practical view?

Just because we can add crypto-tech does not mean that the DAO will be successful.

Although it is possible to aim for a DAO from day one of planning, it is also possible to evolve towards it, and it is equally feasible to incorporate parts of a DAO construct into a traditional organization. If the DAO is the actual nirvana in terms of autonomous agents doing their work through artificial intelligence or smart programs, then we could imagine a path to an evolutionary sequence, where each subsequent stage builds on the functions of the previous one, according to the following evolution:

- **Participative** – users voluntarily and independently participate in loose tasks
- **Collaborative** – users collaborate and add value towards common goals or objectives
- **Cooperative** – users expect some shared gains to be returned
- **Distributed** – starts the propagation of these functions by multiplying them across a wider net
- **Decentralized** – further scalability is reached by instilling more powers to the edges
- **Autonomous** – autonomous agents, smart programs, and (later) increased levels of artificial intelligence and AI algorithms provide self-sustainability in operations and value creation at the centers, edges, and arteries of an organization.

There are various pieces that you need to think about in a methodical manner, as an implementation checklist that you gradually tackle:

1. *What Scope?* The users are at the center of this evolution, and so is the architectural backbone to support these user actions. Note that the participative, collaborative, cooperative functions are user-based, whereas the distributed, decentralized, autonomous ones are architecture-based.

2. *Types of Ownership Stake.* There are three ways to be involved in a DAO. You can buy shares, cryptocurrency, or tokens; they can be granted to you; or you can earn them. The earning part is interesting because it involves some work that is active or passive. An example of active working includes delivering on bounties for specific projects such as finding bugs, developing software, ethical hacking, or any task that is required by the DAO. Passive working is typically accomplished by sharing something, such as your computer processing cycles, Internet access, storage, or even your data.

3. *Units of Value.* What you receive in return for your stake can also take many forms. Of course, the traditional instrument is a share (or a warrant/option for shares), but value can also come in points, tokens, rewards or a cryptocurrency. Note that tokens could have multiple purposes, as they can represent product usage rights or ownership rights tied to some intrinsic value.

4. *Transparency in Governance.* Getting governance right is not easy, but it must be done. Autonomy does not imply anarchy, so you'll need to think about the various parts that make up governance, whether or not stakeholders are involved actively (e.g., voting, managing, creating rules, checking rules, decision-making, reporting, regulations),

or passively (e.g., feeling empowered, valued, respected, fairly compensated[2]). Regardless, transparency in governance must prevail.

5. *Gains Appreciation.* In the traditional sense, we have had profit sharing or dividend participation as a form of collective gain redistribution. But in a DAO these benefits might include voting/special rights, or being given a special status. Ultimately, there has to be value growth happening through internal capital appreciation, either in the form of cryptocurrency or cryptographically secure tokenization of some sort.

6. *Crypto-based Technology.* The blockchain and cryptocurrency-based protocols and platforms are just enablers for the consensus mechanism. Typically, these are open source decentralized consensus and decentralized trust protocols that enable the irrefutability, verifiability and veracity of all transactions and smart programs. These protocols can be general purpose (e.g., Ethereum, Bitcoin), or special purpose (e.g., La'ZooZ for decentralized transportation or MaidSafe for decentralized storage). There are three additional functional components that should be included in the technology platform: a) a user data layer, with an assumption that data is owned by the user, and only accessible in a specific aggregate or blind form by the DAO, b) smart programs which are the actual transaction engines, and c) various application program interfaces (APIs) to interface with value-added services or partners that are ancillary to a DAO.

A key objective of a DAO is value creation or production, and to make that happen, there needs to be a specific linkage between user actions and the resulting effects of those actions on the overall value to the organization, as symbolized by the value of the cryptocurrency that is underlying it. That is where entrepreneurial creativity needs to take place, and where business models will be concocted.

Usage without value linkage is a waste, and will result in a failure backlash. Yes, this is a a warning. Many of these DAOs will be theoretical in their inception stages. A cryptocurrency crowdsale only enables the DAO to start on a path. At the end of the day, a new DAO is like a startup. It requires a product/market fit, business model realization, and a lot of users (customers) to move forward. Early on, a lot of assumptions are made, and the DAO may resemble a science fiction project, until the product or service hits the reality of market forces that decide its viability. The "proof of success" will be sustainability in the market, not the crowdfunding success.

Despite its coveted status, getting to a DAO is a step-by-step, gradual building block process that cannot be artificially accelerated. A DAC/DAO has degrees of purity in its implementation. There will be cases where only a percentage of a company is a DAC or operates like one.

LIGHTHOUSE INDUSTRIES

Governments and Governance

Governments and governance-related applications are ripe for blockchain technology. We categorize them in three segments:

1. Existing jurisdictions in national, state, provincial, county, city or municipality settings
2. Virtual governance for nations or organizations
3. Board governance for companies

Existing "brick and mortar" governments who move some of their services to the blockchain will see it as an evolution from the current e-services being offered.

SOME BLOCKCHAIN-BASED SERVICES FOR TRADITIONAL GOVERNMENTS	
• Marriage registration	• Property ownership
• Procurement auctions	• Motor vehicle registration
• Passport issuance	• Patents
• Benefits collection	• Taxes
• Land registration	• Voting
• Licenses	• Government bonds
• Birth certificates	• Filings and compliance

However, governments will take a long time to implement these services. They will undoubtedly start by analyzing the full impact and ramifications of such projects, then evaluate the scalability requirements. The bar will be very high on their expectations, because government services cannot fail, once launched. Smaller countries, counties or cities may have an advantage in trying early projects, as they avoid potential blockchain scalability limitations.

With virtual governance, BitNation offers an example of what is possible. It is a DIY smorgasbord covering legal, insurance, social, security, and diplomacy services. It includes a global public notary service where anyone can record their legal documents on the blockchain, and file them by permanently time-stamping their existence on the blockchain.

Estonia has implemented the BitNation public notary service. For example, If a couple gets married on the BitNation public notary,[3] it does not mean they get married in the jurisdiction of Estonia, or in any other jurisdiction. They get married only in the "blockchain jurisdiction."[4]

Ukraine is pioneering a blockchain-based election platform (on Ethereum) that will allow multiple levels of elections, including political primaries, elections, online petitions or referenda.[5]

For traditional companies, BoardRoom[6] is an out-of-the-box board governance platform that relies on the blockchain to manage decentralized consensus with table proposals that can be voted on and executed through democratic assembly. One of its most interesting features is a direct linkage from governance decision-making to funds clearing. Says Nick Dodson, its creator, "It allows funds to be disbursed to a recipient party, based on pre-set rules, as soon as a vote passes a resolution, cutting the time it takes to get paid from several weeks to instant clearing."

If you want to incorporate your company and run its governance affairs on the blockchain, Otonomos[7] lets you "order" a new company in Singapore, Hong Kong or the United Kingdom. You can allocate share capital to shareholders, appoint directors, issue options to employees, or convertible notes to investors (via smart contracts) from the convenience of a dashboard and without touching a piece of paper.

There is another potential application of DIY Government 2.0. Suppose a country's real government is failing, concerned citizens could create a shadow blockchain governance that is more fair, decentralized and accountable. There are at least 50 failed, fragile, or corrupt states that could benefit from an improved blockchain governance.[8]

Health Care

When we look at the healthcare industry spectrum, it is tempting to presume that the blockchain's capabilities are going to be a silver bullet that will fix the challenges with medical records and patient data privacy.

Compiling a transportable, yet integrated medical record is an old and hard problem to solve. We cannot expect the blockchain to address all the issues related to health care and technology. The regulatory hurdles are not to be underestimated, especially if blockchain approaches create a conflict with the current laws.

The theory is attractive: publish your medical record safely on the blockchain and be assured that you or an authorized person can access it anywhere in the world. That is what the government of Estonia has done—a good case of blockchain technology in healthcare. Using Guardtime's large scale keyless data authentication, in combination with a distributed ledger, citizens carry their ID credentials which unlock access to their healthcare records in real-time. From that point forward, the blockchain ensures a clear chain of custody, and it keeps a register of anyone who touches these records, while ensuring that compliance process is maintained.[9]

Other healthcare usages might include:

- Using a combination of multisignature processes and QR codes, we can grant specific access of our medical record or parts of it, to authorized healthcare providers.
- Sharing our patient data in the aggregate, while anonymizing it to ensure privacy is maintained. This is helpful in research, and for comparing similar cases against one another.
- Recording and time-stamping delivery of medical procedures or events, in order to reduce insurance fraud, facilitate compliance and verification of services being rendered.
- Recording the maintenance history of critical pieces of medical equipment, for example, an MRI scanner, providing a permanent audit trail.
- Carrying a secure wallet with our full electronic medical record in it, or our stored DNA, and allowing its access, in case of emergency.
- Verifying provenance on medications, to eliminate illegal drug manufacturing.
- "CaseCoins:" originating specific altcoins that create a cryptocurrency market around solving a particular disease, such as FoldingCoin, a project where participants share their processing power to help cure a disease, and get rewarded with a token asset.[10]

Energy

Blockchain applications can help achieve a more efficient management of the power distribution grid, low-cost microtransactions between peers or machines, secondary markets creation, or rule-based payments.

RWE, a German energy company, is looking at connecting electric vehicles charging stations to a blockchain (via Slock.it, which is running on Ethereum). This service allows users to charge their cars and pay in microtransaction slices. The charging station handles user authentication, payment processing and loyalty point assignments as part of one single immutable transaction. This simplifies the billing and provides simpler accounting, an existing bottleneck in the energy market.[11]

TransActive Grid, a joint venture of LO3 Energy and ConsenSys, has developed a business logic layer that delivers real-time metering of local energy generation, enabling residents to buy and sell renewable energy to their neighbours. The first demonstration of this project took place in March 2016, in a Brooklyn, New York neighborhood between 10 customers, and received interest from 130 others.[12]

Accenture has revealed a proof-of-concept of a smart plug prototype that works with other house gadgets that monitor power use. When demand is high or low it searches for energy prices and then uses the modified blockchain to switch suppliers if it finds a cheaper source. It could help many people on lower incomes who pay for their power via a meter.[13]

Grid Singularity[14] is experimenting with the blockchain to authenticate energy transactions. The company is targeting developing countries, where it wants to make pay-as-you-go solar more secure. Its eventual goal is to build a blockchain platform for energy systems that can be applied to any type of transaction on the grid.

KEY IDEAS FROM CHAPTER FIVE

1. The story of the blockchain's impact will not be complete until it propagates further into a variety of industries, government, and horizontal cases.

2. While the blockchain chips away at some functions from existing intermediaries, it also enables the creation of new players.

3. Soon, we will be able to get a "proof for everything," as easily as google searching for everything.

4. Outside financial services, government, health care and energy are the next potential industries that will experience increased activity in blockchain-based innovation.

5. Distributed Autonomous Organizations (DAOs) are an important application of the blockchain, but their practical implementation is still in its early stages.

NOTES

1. "Bitcoin and the Three Laws of Robotics, Let's Talk Bitcoin," https://letstalkbitcoin.com/bitcoin-and-the-three-laws-of-robotics#.UjjO0mTFT7v, 2013.

2. "Do Peers Really Want to Govern Their Platforms?," Brad Burnham, Union Square Ventures, https://www.usv.com/post/54c7abcd570e2300033262e6/do-peers-really-want-to-govern-their-platforms, 2015.

3. BitNation Public Notary (BPN), https://bitnation.co/notary/.

4. "Bitnation and Estonian Government Start Spreading Sovereign Jurisdiction on the Blockchain," IB Times, Ian Allison, http://www.ibtimes.co.uk/bitnation-estonian-government-start-spreading-sovereign-jurisdiction-blockchain-1530923, November 2015.

5. "Ukraine Government Plans to Trial Ethereum Blockchain-Based Election Platform," Bitcoin Magazine, https://bitcoinmagazine.com/articles/ukraine-government-plans-to-trial-ethereum-blockchain-based-election-platform-1455641691, February 2016.

6. BoardRoom, http://boardroom.to/.

7. Otonomos, otonomos.com.

8. List of countries by Fragile States Index, Wikipedia, https://en.wikipedia.org/wiki/List_of_countries_by_Fragile_States_Index.

9. "Guartime Secures over a Million Estonian Healthcare Records on the Blockchain," Ian Allison, IB Times, http://www.ibtimes.co.uk/guardtime-secures-over-million-estonian-healthcare-records-blockchain-1547367, March 2016.

10. "Blockchain in Healthcare: From Theory to Reality," Jonathan Cordwell, http://blogs.csc.com/2015/10/30/blockchain-in-healthcare-from-theory-to-reality/.

11. "Partnering with RWE to Explore the Future of the Energy Sector," Stephan Tual, https://blog.slock.it/partnering-with-rwe-to-explore-the-future-of-the-energy-sector-1cc89b9993e6#.w3oj745sc.

12. "Blockchain-based Microgrid Gives Power to Consumers in New York," New Scientist, https://www.newscientist.com/article/2079334-blockchain-based-microgrid-gives-power-to-consumers-in-new-york/, March 2016.

13. "Bitcoin Could Help Cut Power Bills," BBC, http://www.bbc.com/news/technology-35604674.

14. Grid Singularity, http://gridsingularity.com/.

□-□-⑥-□-□

IMPLEMENTING BLOCKCHAIN TECHNOLOGY

"Imagination is more important than knowledge. For knowledge is limited to all we now know and understand, while imagination embraces the entire world."

—ALBERT EINSTEIN

THE MORE FOUNDATIONAL A TECHNOLOGY IS, the more impact it can have. Blockchain technology is not a process improvement technology. At its fullest deployment potential, it is rather a disruptive technology; therefore it must be given that potential when being implemented.

Most of the major blockchain platforms have been developed via a transparent, open source, collaborative approach, including a good degree of decentralized contributed work. This has two outcomes: a) the proverbial "sausage-making" is not always pretty, and b) up until final releases are set, implementation and deployment compromises are more routine than exceptions. Until blockchain technology development matures (around 2018–2020), you will need to manage the variety of implementation challenges that are paved along its way.

We could end up with a similar situation as during the Web's initial years. Many early businesses failed, some due to weaknesses in technology, others due to stretched business model assumptions (the result of a lack of enough market experience), and some due to both. Eventually, Internet and Web technology evolved, improved, and enabled the building of more powerful implementations.

With the blockchain, one could adopt a conservative approach and wait until the technology matures, then get involved when all uncertainties are removed. As the saying goes, the early bird would get the worm, but the second mouse gets the cheese. Some companies will undoubtedly follow that route, while others will be more attracted to being pioneers and innovators who are willing to trade risks for greater or earlier rewards.

There are two ongoing approaches for implementing the blockchain: a) inside existing organizations, as an add-on technology; or b) outside organizations, by a startup who may not be as concerned with existing processes. This chapter focuses on covering early steps in internal blockchain implementations, inside organizations. Many of the ideas in Chapters 3, 4, and 5 highlighted the innovative work of startups. Later in this chapter, we will also cover inter-organizational opportunities that are a mix of the former two.

INTERNAL STRATEGIES FOR TACKLING THE BLOCKCHAIN

There is no right or wrong way to implement the blockchain within large organizations. There are various approaches. A startup begins with a blank sheet of paper, and no baggage. But an organization can be held hostage by its existing situation. The old adage, "Yes, God created the world in six days, but that's because he didn't have an installed base," is true again.

Getting large organizations up to speed and knowledgeable about blockchains and their impact is not an overnight project.

It takes some time before a given issue (the blockchain) gains momentum, understanding, and share of mind within senior executive ranks, along the way in figuring on the CEO's priority agenda. Typically, that starts to happen after a combination of groundswell interest from progressive employees, and via external market pressures.

Suddenly, one or a handful of employees in leadership positions begin owning the blockchain topic, and they start to continuously think about it. Some of the organizational questions might be:

- How shall we organize to tackle the blockchain, and why?
- How do we develop use cases, strategies and implementation approaches?
- How do we evolve from Proofs of Concepts to full deployments?
- What documented benefits shall we be expecting from the blockchain—strategic versus operational?
- What lessons are we learning, and mistakes are we making?
- What benchmarks are we measuring ourselves against?
- What best practices can we share, so we can be more effective in our endeavours?
- What can we hope to accomplish over the next year?

THE BLOCKCHAIN CZAR

The origin of the czar analogy dates back to the reengineering days during the early 1990s when Michael Hammer and James Champy advocated the role of the "reengineering czar" in their book, *Reenginering the Corporation*. The reengineering czar was that person who would become the rallying point for reengineering efforts within a company.

In the reengineering definition, the reengineering czar is "an individual responsible for developing reengineering techniques and tools within the company and for achieving synergy across the company's separate reengineering projects."[1]

It is noteworthy that the reengineering czar does not make reengineering "happen." That is the role of "reengineering leaders" who receive support from the czar. Continuing on the role of the reengineering czar from Hammer and Champy, "The reengineering czar has two main functions: one, enabling and supporting each individual process owner and reengineering team, and two, coordinating all ongoing reengineering activities."

In my last year at Hewlett-Packard in 1995, I held the role of Reengineering Czar for the company's Canadian Operations. That position reported to the CEO because reengineering was an executive level initiative that had the highest possible level of agenda priority. At that time, I was managing a dozen reengineering projects by assisting the teams that were implementing them across the company, and we followed Hammer and Champy's methods and practices, with great success.

For historical reference, there is a governmental related antecedent to the czar positions. In 1993, President Clinton appointed Ira Magaziner[2] as the United States Internet Czar, during a time when there were 11 czar titles nominated by the White House. It is interesting to note that the number of czar titles later skyrocketed to 33 under President George W. Bush (2001–2009) and 38 under President Barack Obama (2009–2016).[3]

The difference between the reengineering days and the early blockchain period is that the "cookbook" for reengineering was largely written, and much of the work was about implementation. In the early 1990s, the underlying catalyst technology was Information Technology, and it was stable, unlike enterprise blockchain technologies that were still growing and maturing as of 2016. However, the spirit and intent of the reengineering czar position remains totally applicable for the blockchain.

Following the practices of process reengineering was business religion in its purest form, and it is my hope that blockchain initiatives and investments get the same treatment.

In this context, the "Blockchain Czar" should have experience in your own business operations and they should understand the role of reengineering business processes via technology implementations. This person could also become the company internal and external spokesperson. Ideally, this role is not to be filled by an analyst from the research department, but they could be part of an innovation group, as long as they have had operational experience. The Blockchain Czar will be responsible for removing obstacles within your organization, facilitating education, curating and sharing best practices, and overseeing the progress of various implementations across the organization. This job is a tough one, because it involves finding and obliterating old processes, instead of automating or streamlining what is currently being done.

ORGANIZATIONAL MODELS

So, how do you organize internally? There are various options.

Some companies are funding a "Blockchain Labs" entity that includes software engineers who can get their "hands dirty," as soon as ideas come to the fore and need to be demonstrated. These labs typically have an internal focus to "show and sell," or educate the blockchain's possibilities to other business units and departments within the organization. Their challenge is typically not in the incubation of ideas, but rather in how these ideas get handed over and implemented inside other departments and business units who are the real implementation playgrounds.

Some other organizations have formed an internal blockchain task force comprised of the various business unit stakeholders, who meet and communicate on a regular basis. The challenge with this type of approach is that not all of these stakeholders may be at the same level of knowledge or motivation and they may not agree on a given direction. The role of this group could be more about sharing and collective learning than influencing.

Another approach is to discover ideas within the various groups via a common process, but to develop the proofs of concepts for them in the labs, then proceed to implementing the best candidates with the business units.

Regardless of the approach, they would all benefit from at least one strong blockchain advocate that is a respected thought leader, a bold communicator, and an enthusiast about blockchain technologies.

A BLOCKCHAIN FUNCTIONAL ARCHITECTURE

One way to understand the scope of blockchains is by studying the comprehensive functionality they hold. This section depicts a proposed generic building block approach that was derived by analyzing the various approaches that exist on the market.

In 2016, it looks like these pieces are many, but there will be consolidation, and we will gradually start to talk less about what is under the hood, and more in terms of higher-up capabilities. Eventually, this type of technology infrastructure will be taken for granted, and most of it will come assembled "out-of-the-box," instead of in an IKEA box, like the early approaches.

The following are the building blocks of a blockchain technology:

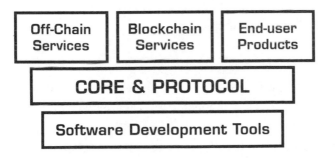

Let us dive inside each one of these pieces in more detail.

CORE & PROTOCOL

Peer-to-Peer Network

The Peer-to-Peer (P2P) Network is the collection of computers that are connected together as nodes, and into an ever expanding topology. It is a basic foundational element of a blockchain. Each node runs the same software, therefore delivering inherent redundancies to the whole network, which means that if one node goes down, or is not responding, the work of other nodes is always compensating. In essence, a P2P network is difficult to take down entirely. You would have to take each and every node down.

Consensus Algorithm

The various methods that dictate "what" or "how many" nodes can participate in the permissioning aspects of validating transactions is also part of the consensus algorithm configuration, and they help to determine if the outcome is a public, private or semi-private form of consensus. Mining may or may not be involved in this process. Keys and signatures are part of this functionality.

The early years of blockchain developments were plagued with heated discussions over which type of consensus is best, but as these technologies mature, and certainly past 2018, the type of consensus algorithm will be a moot subject, as it will be taken for granted, as long as it is efficient, secure, and well supported.

Virtual Machine

It is a concept, borrowed by the popular Java Virtual Machine (JVM) approach, but pioneered by Ethereum, within the blockchain development context. The Virtual Machine depicts the part of the protocol that handles internal state and computation. It can be thought of as a large decentralized computer (actually made-up of the several P2P machines) that contains information about the millions of accounts, which update an internal database, execute code, and interact with one another. Programs written in Smart Contract Language get compiled into the Virtual Machine, and to create the contracts you send the transaction containing your code.

Historical Record

Transactions are actually recorded in sequential data blocks (hence the word blockchain), so there is a historical, append-only log of these transactions that is continuously maintained and updated. A fallacy is that the blockchain is a distributed ledger. In the technical sense, it is not, but it acts as one, because the collection of transactions on blocks is equivalent to a distributed ledger. However, you can build immutable distributed ledger applications based on the historical records that the blockchain provides.

State Balances

Bitcoin was not designed around accounts, although accounts are a more common way to think about the transactions that are taking place, because we are used to looking at our banking transactions as such. Under the hood, Bitcoin uses a method called Unspent Transaction Outputs (UTXO), a concept that links unspent transactions as an output that can be spent as an input in a new transaction. Other blockchains use different methods to keep tracks of state balance. Ripple has a ledger that contains a snapshot of the current balances held everywhere on the network as opposed to a chain of historical events. In Ethereum, the state is made up of objects called "accounts," with each account having state transitions being direct transfers of value and information between accounts.

A GENERIC APPROACH TO BLOCKCHAIN FUNCTIONALITY

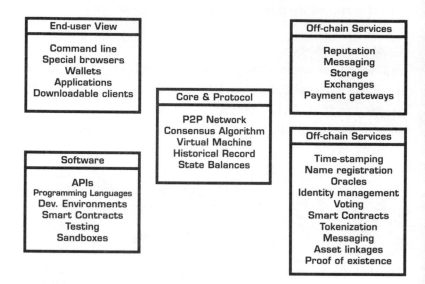

BLOCKCHAIN SOFTWARE DEVELOPMENT

The various pieces comprising blockchain software development include:

- APIs (Applications Programming Interfaces)
- Various client implementations (e.g., C++, Python, Go, Java, Haskell)
- Integrated Development Environments and Rapid Application Development frameworks
- Smart Contract Languages and Scripts
- Testing tools
- Sandbox environments

ON-CHAIN SERVICES

- Time-stamping
- Naming registration
- Oracles
- Identity management (online, legal, pseudo, etc.)
- Voting
- Smart Contract Management
- Tokenization
- Messaging
- Assets linkages
- Proof of existence

END-USER VIEW

- Command line
- Special browsers
- Wallets
- Applications
- Downloadable clients (as the application entry point)

OFF-CHAIN SERVICES

- Reputation
- Messaging
- Storage (DHTs, File systems)
- Exchanges (for tokens, assets, currency)
- Payments gateways

OTHER DESIRED BLOCKCHAIN FEATURES

- Encrypted transactions (confidential transmissions)
- Monitoring (statistics and analysis)
- Audit
- Security

WRITING DECENTRALIZED APPLICATIONS

Since the consensus process of blockchains is decentralized by nature, it makes sense they are enabling a new breed of decentralized applications. A decentralized app can be decentralized technically, politically, or both.

The reality is that decentralized apps are not for everything, and not everything fits a decentralized app paradigm. However, there are a lot of applications that do fit the blockchain distributed paradigm, and that presents a good amount of opportunities for developers, creators, and visionaries.

Decentralized applications start by creating their own rules for ownerships, transaction requirements, and logic.

There are various levels of sophistication in writing decentralized applications.

1. Use cryptocurrency as a currency unit to pay for services.
2. Use a blockchain service as a feature, for example, to register an asset or verify the authenticity of a process, typically done via an API.
3. Use a smart contract on a blockchain to run some business logic that returns a particular value if certain conditions are met, for example, financial derivatives. In this case, there's a digital asset whose ownership and movement are governed by the blockchain.
4. Use the blockchain in a more fundamental way, where the app would not function without the blockchain. Typically, you would set-up a specific peer-to-peer network with nodes, for example, OpenBazaar, as a decentralized e-commerce app.
5. Use your own blockchain (could be shared with others), without an economic token or currency unit. This is where most of the permissioned blockchains play within enterprises.

6. Use your own blockchain (or another blockchain), including a token or currency unit, to create an economic network of value, for example, MaidSafe,[3] which creates a market for unused computing resources over a peer-to-peer network of users.

12 FEATURES OF A BLOCKCHAIN PLATFORM

If you need to evaluate a given blockchain platform, the following features are important:

1. **Programmability.** What specific programming languages are available?
2. **Scalability.** How many nodes can the blockchain grow? Will there be upper limits?
3. **Upgradability.** What is the track record of the developers for delivering enhancements and upgrades to the blockchain?
4. **Transactions manageability.** Is there real-time transparency for all transactions?
5. **Visibility.** Do you have a full view on the blockchain activity?
6. **Affordability.** What is the cost of deploying that technology?
7. **Security.** What is the documented confidence level in the blockchain's security?
8. **Speed/Performance.** What are the upper limits for speed in validating transactions?
9. **High Availability.** What is the uptime's track record?
10. **Extensibility.** Can you extend the basic blockchain functionality with a variety of add-ons?
11. **Interoperability.** Does it inter-operate well with other blockchains or related technologies?
12. **Open Source.** Is the code open source? What is the level of collaboration and contributions from a variety of developers?

Issue 1: Blockchain Redefines Legacy

Large companies are always battling with their legacy applications, because these can be anchors that drag them when new technologies arrive. Even when you thought corporate IT was safe with modern software environments that make use of modular cloud-based capabilities, container-based technology to facilitate operations deployments, or continuous delivery with agile and rapid developments practices, the blockchain is yet another "modern technology" that will need to be absorbed and integrated into the technology toolset of any software development teams.

Issue 2: Blockchain is a Strategic IT Platform

As clearly mentioned in Chapter 1, and expanded upon earlier in this chapter, the blockchain, in its fullest form, is a new major software development platform. Therefore, it is becoming increasingly strategic. Strategic means that it is not just there to reduce costs and improve transactions latency. Strategic means that it needs to find strategic usages that can give you a competitive advantage. Specifically, the intersection of private and public blockchains will yield some very innovative applications, but that exploitation will only become possible when internal organizations are at par with the advancements in applying public blockchain technology.

Issue 3: What Competencies?

There are 5 categories of competencies required to fully roll out blockchain solutions within a company: Education, Discovery, Design, Development and Management.

Education: Learning the basic functionality of a blockchain, and what it enables generically.

Discovery: Identification of areas of opportunities by answering where does the blockchain fit, and what can we do with it?

Design: What solutions functionality will we need to address the potential we saw in the discovery phase? How will it affect what we are doing, including the business process, contractual and legal requirements?

Development: Software development, integration, and deployment of the technology.

Management: Ongoing software maintenance, support, iterative evolution, new features, and updates.

**WHAT BLOCKCHAIN COMPETENCIES
DO YOU HAVE?**

Most companies cannot develop expertise in all of these areas, but they may partner with outside firms for specific aspects of these steps. Knowing how to program blockchains will be a required competency, just as important as programming Web Apps.

Issue 4: What Partners to Choose?

Every organization sits at a different starting point, based on their resources and capabilities, so the chosen approach will rest with your particular situation. The following table segments the various approaches:

APPROACH	HOW IT'S DONE	EXAMPLES
IT Services	We will build you anything	Big IT firms
Blockchain	You work directly with the blockchain's tools and services	Bitcoin, Ethereum
Development Platforms	Frameworks for IT professionals	Eris, BlockApps
Solutions	Industry-specific	Clearmatics, DAH, Chain
APIs & Overlays	DIY assembling pieces	Open Assets, Tierion

Issue 5: Back-end Integrations

When blockchain applications start to reach full deployment levels, they will eventually need to integrate with a variety of back-end systems, just as customer-facing Web and mobile applications had to integrate with existing enterprise systems. However, the blockchain also has the potential to replace some back-end processes, so you must take that likely scenario into account. But keep in mind that it will be easier to start implementing blockchain solutions in some new segments, without internal integrations. If your starting position includes your current systems, then you are inherently extending your implementation horizon by potentially as long as an extra 18–24 months. So, why not consider starting with no baggage and earn new customers who want to try something new?

Issue 6: Blockchain as a Shared Services Platform

In addition to internal applications and use cases, there will be a number of new opportunities for creating shared blockchain services, either at the vertical level (e.g., a particular financial services application), or at the horizontal level (e.g., a generic records verification service).

Issue 7: Disrupt or Construct?

For startups, there is no doubt the blockchain is a disruptor, but large companies do not like to disrupt themselves unless they are forced to. Within large companies, the first likely scenarios will be to deploy blockchain technology to strengthen their existing operations, by achieving new levels of efficiency or seeing cost reductions. However, it may not be enough. The specter of outside disruption will still loom if you stop short at the constructive/defensive stages.

Issue 8: Blockchain As the New Database

The blockchain as a database is a recurring theme in this book, so you might as well have as many blockchain-savvy developers as you have database-savvy developers. Knowing when to use a traditional database and when to use a blockchain will be important, and knowing how to optimize their dual operations will be even more important.

Issue 9: Blockchain Platforms

In 2016, we are seeing many pieces and choices, and "hand assembly" is still required. We may be in similar stages as when we had to build Web pages by writing HTML code, page by page. Blockchains that come out of the box will be a welcomed evolution, although Blockchain-as-a-Service is a step in that direction.

Issue 10: How to Get Educated

You can take a proactive approach to educating various departments about blockchain technology, or you can wait until the market continues to educate everybody generically. If there is no sense of urgency, it probably means that either you have not taken the time to understand the full potential of the blockchain, or that the blockchain effort is not being led by the right person whose job will be to light-up the required sparks within the various business units.

Issue 11: Dead-End vs. End-to-End Proofs of Concept

Proof of Concepts (POCs) are popular in some large companies, as a way to dip your toes into new technology without getting totally wet. But the risks are that they could be timid experiments that do not show commitments and they might reach a dead-end, because they will not always allow you to see the potential benefits. It's better to implement smaller blockchain projects end-to-end where you can see results and a full lifecycle of usage with real users. That said, POCs can be used to narrow down a portfolio of committed projects, but you need to move beyond them.

Issue 12: Business Process vs. Technology

I have long argued that implementing the blockchain is 80% about business process changes and 20% about figuring out the technology behind it. Of course, this assumes that you want to be ambitious enough to tackle the required toughness in changing business processes. If you think that the blockchain technology is not ready yet, or has some weaknesses that might be solved later, then use that time to start reengineering your business process, and by the time you are done the technology will be ready.

Issue 13: Use Cases Saturation

Brainstorming to find use cases is good as an initial entry point, but it is not enough. The risk is in thinking that use cases are disposables. You try them, and if you do not like them, you throw them out. Use cases could lead to something, or maybe not. The term "use case" assumes that something has to fit within existing processes, so the bar is not high enough for making more difficult choices that go beyond the obvious, and into the innovation discovery potential. The next section tackles how to think about the blockchain with an innovation hat on.

DECISION-MAKING FRAMEWORK

Often, the first question that comes to mind is: "What problem is the blockchain solving?" It is a good, but self-limiting question, because it assumes that the blockchain can only solve known problems.

What if the blockchain could create new opportunities, instead of solving existing problems? Then, you will need a different mindset to take that direction. The Internet did start by solving specific problems that world trade was complaining about, but it provided us electronic commerce as a novel version of global trade. If you asked the newspapers, they didn't think they had any problems, but the Internet challenged their industry. Social media was not a solution to a problem, but an enhancement on human relations.

We could categorize the blockchain's impact into three broad categories:

1. Solving Problems
2. Creating Opportunities
3. Applying Capabilities

Solving Problems

The "problems" category comes in a variety of flavors. It forces the thinking around understanding if the blockchain has immediate applications that could impact:

Cost savings: Back-office? Middle-office? Customer service?
Productivity: More throughput?
Efficiency: Faster processing? Compliance/Reporting enablement?
Time delays: Faster clearing? Faster settlements?
Quality: Less errors? More satisfaction?
Outcomes: Growth in revenues? Increased profits?
Risk: Less fraud? Less exposure?

Although the above is not a list of "problems" in the pure sense of the word, it is a list of fundamental business parameters that any organization wishes to streamline. In this case, the blockchain is an invisible enabler that does not change much to the externally visible parts of a business. Rather, it is more of an internal black box that does something better than before.

Hopefully, you are convinced that just asking what problem the blockchain solves is a limiting question on its own. For example, if you look at the startup innovation around banks in FinTech, you will see plenty of cases where these new companies did not really solve a "problem" the banks had, but they tackled a particular market or service differently. So the tipping point was to compete by reframing the opportunity, for example, peer-to-peer lending, unconventional home loans, really fast approval cycles, efficient robot investing, and so on.

Creating Opportunities

It is more difficult to figure out opportunities, because that requires applying innovation, being creative, and making profound changes. These are more difficult objectives to achieve, because business process changes are involved, and it takes a longer time to change them. When you sum it up, the blockchain is about 80% business process changes, and 20% technology implementation.

Creating new opportunities includes entering new markets and/or providing new services that the blockchain enables and that were not possible before. It requires a more imaginative process of dreaming up what's possible and what wasn't done before. It requires thinking outside the proverbial box, and a deep understanding of what the blockchain can enable in the areas that it is strongly suited for.

New Services Opportunities:

- New Intermediaries
- New Networks
- New Marketplaces
- New Clearinghouses
- New Authorities

These new opportunities could also develop as new markets around 3 spaces: inside your organization, collaboratively between two or several organizations, or in totally new areas that do not initially interface with internal processes. Arguably, anything done on the outside might be easier to tackle because you're not initially tied down by your core integration requirements.

- **Inside:** Can we attract a new segment of customers?
- **Outside:** Can we enter a new market outside of our core?
- **Collaborative:** Is there a white space we can collaborate on?

Applying Capabilities

The third category of thinking involves applying the blockchain's capabilities from the ground-up.

In these cases, a deep understanding of the blockchain's capabilities will lead you to discover implementation ideas for your own business. It's a lot easier for someone to understand the blockchain than for a blockchain person to understand someone's business.

Here's a list of generic capabilities that the blockchain enables:

- Rethinking intermediaries
- Bundling services
- Unbundling services
- New flows of value
- Decentralized governance

- New legal frameworks
- Running smart contracts on the blockchain
- Sharing a distributed ledger
- Creating/Issuing digital assets
- Embedding trust rules inside transactions and interactions
- Time-stamping
- Implementing digital signatures
- Notarizing data/documents to produce proof
- Creating records of a business process, event, or activity
- Verifying authenticity of data/ownership/documents/assets
- Confirming authenticity of transactions
- Ensuring that contractual conditions are undeniably met
- Reconciling accounts
- Finalizing financial settlements
- Embedding digital identity in applications
- Providing escrow or custodial services
- Enabling smart things to transact securely

For example, you cannot directly compare the blockchain to a database and say, "The database does this better therefore we do not need blockchain transactions." The blockchain is a new paradigm. Rather, start by running smart contracts on a blockchain, and ask yourself what it can enable, then work backwards to see how you can tie it back to your business.

When looking at your blockchain strategy, you need to tackle all three elements in parallel: problem solving, opportunities discovery, and capabilities enablement. That's the trinity of sanity for an organizational blockchain strategy.

KEY IDEAS FROM CHAPTER SIX

1. Managing an internal blockchain strategy takes some concerted effort and leadership.

2. The "Blockchain Czar" approach is an effective method for booting-up and coordinating disparate efforts in large organizations.

3. A blockchain implementation will have a number of new architectural and functional components that need to work in harmony.

4. Companies will need to decide what implementation approaches to choose, based on their own competencies and choice of external partnerships.

5. You should not just see the Blockchain as a problem-solving technology. Rather, it is a technology that lets you innovate and target new opportunities.

NOTES

1. Ira Magaziner, https://en.wikipedia.org/wiki/Ira_Magaziner.
2. "List of U.S. executive branch czars," https://en.wikipedia.org/wiki/List_of_U.S._executive_branch_czars.
3. MaidSafe, http://maidsafe.net/.

☐-☐-7-☐-☐

DECENTRALIZATION AS THE
WAY FORWARD

"All things are difficult before they're easy."

—THOMAS FULLER

A DECENTRALIZED TECHNOLOGY (the blockchain) will telegraph a decentralized world.

If we thought the blockchain's destiny was just to infiltrate enterprise systems and replace intermediaries, think again. That was only the beginning. The blockchain's *raison d'être* is to enable us to imagine a new world that will be largely decentralized.

Decentralization does not mean anarchy or performing illegal acts. It means that an individual user is more empowered and less restricted. It implies that many contributors, many beneficiaries, and many leaders are working in harmony. It is neither communism nor a version of cyberpunk fiction. Decentralization boosts capitalism by creating new layers of work production and value creation.

It is granted that a blockchain will move value. But go further and start imagining multiple blockchains interacting with one another, all of them trading value with one another, and you will be led to a composite of network effects, potentially more significant than the previous generation of network effects. It will be the equivalent of a huge overlay of decentralized services that are open and accessible to anyone.

Maybe the blockchain will lead us to the not-so utopian view of Nobel Prize winner, economist, and philosopher, Friedrich Hayek. He believed that the path to a functioning economy—or society— was decentralization, and asserted that a decentralized economy complements the dispersed nature of information spread throughout society.[1]

WHAT HAPPENED TO THE DECENTRALIZED INTERNET?

Let us remember the intended vision of the Internet. It was very much about openness in decentralization and distribution of services, with minute controls at the centers. At the dawn of the Internet life in 1994, Kevin Kelly wrote in his book, *Out of Control*, three important comments to remember:

The network is the icon of the 21st century.

The net icon has no center—it is a bunch of dots connected to other dots.

A decentralized, redundant organization can flex without distorting its function, and thus it can adapt.

No wonder Tim Berners-Lee, the inventor of the Web, started an initiative, Web We Want,[2] to reclaim some of the original goals of the Web. Notes Berners-Lee and the website's community:

We are concerned about the growing number of threats to the very existence of the open Web, such as censorship, surveillance, and concentrations of power.

The Web that drives economic progress and knowledge, is the one where anyone can create websites to share culture and information. It's the Web where new businesses bloom, where government transparency is a reality, and where citizens document injustice.

Wow. What Kevin Kelly and Web We Want are saying is pure music to the ears of today's believers that a more decentralized Internet can shepherd us into a better future.

If you are content with the Web today, stop and think for a minute whether you are happy with this situation. Web We Want observes:

Millions of spam blogs and websites are visited by bots to cash in on ads. Even quality websites are so overloaded with automated ads and trackers that using an ad blocker is the only responsible way to surf the Web. Every click is monitored and monetized, and we are pushed to consume more and more repetitive content.

What happened to the Web being a public good?

The blockchain symbolizes a shift in power from the centers to the edges of the networks. This is a vision that we have romanced in the early days of the Internet, but a re-decentralization of the Web could actually happen this time.

Some see the world as being pinned down by trust-controlling central authorities. Others see it more democratized, flatter and resting on new governance models that strike a better balance between center and edge control. The blockchain favors that better balance, and enables it to grow.

Forget the Internet for a minute, and see how we reacted to the financial crisis of 2008. The natural response of policy makers was to overshoot with more regulation. U.S., European, and Asian regulators dictated a consolidation of regulatory agencies, resulting in further centralization of post-trade in the over-the-counter derivatives markets, reducing that oversight to a single point of failure. The Dodd-Frank's[3] mandatory central counterparty clearing provisions were a heavy-handed policy that actually amplified systemic risk, instead of reducing it. As a result, central counterparty clearinghouses have become a new class of "too big to fail" institutions, whereas, ironically, they were previously more widely distributed.

In a 2012 *New York Times* article titled "Stabilization Will not Save Us," Nassim Nicholas Taleb, author of *Antifragile* and *The Black Swan*, opined: "In decentralized systems, problems can be solved early and when they are small."[4]

Indeed, not only was the Web hijacked with too many central choke points, regulators supposedly continue to centralize controls in order to lower risk, whereas the opposite should be done.

IT'S NOT EASY BEING DECENTRALIZED

Apple's iTunes is a typical centralized marketplace. If it were decentralized, Apple would not fancy a 30% commission on sales. Instead, app publishers could spread their distribution and marketing costs in a decentralized manner, and Apple would not deserve that 30% to choke the access and search points. Of course, this is a hypothetical scenario, but the nugget of thought behind it is that the value is at the edges of the network, not at its center.

Technically speaking, search and discovery is not a central specific function, and the same experience could be delivered in a distributed manner. Nothing happens without users that add value, so why not recirculate a part of that value back into the network to make it stronger? New decentralized applications are being built on the blockchain, and they do not require a central toll-based app store structure.

It's not easy to become decentralized if you were not designed that way. But it's easier if you start being decentralized from the ground up, as a decentralized network, platform, service, product, currency, or marketplace.

WHAT WILL DECENTRALIZATION LOOK LIKE

It used to be that nothing happened without central authorities, central powers, central regulations, or central approvals. With decentralization, the tables are turned. A lot happens at the edges, and at the nodes near the peripheries of the overall network.

The concept of "central operations" is shattered, because maybe it does not exist. An underlying decentralized protocol (like OpenBazaar for commerce) enables decentralized operations at the edges of the network, and that is where the activity and value resides.

It is completely possible to build a system where value starts with the users who are the key actors in a decentralized organism. If users benefit, then the network benefits collectively, and it spills over to the original creators of the network.

With decentralization, you do not install a center first. You first install a platform that enables the network to flourish where the "center" of attention (used figuratively) interconnects nodes of activity among peripheral users. Then, you build your business model on the shoulders of that initial construct. For example, what used to be a paid option in the old central version might be free in the decentralized version, but you will have the opportunity to create new monetization methods that are more organic to the decentralization itself.

We should not compromise on the decentralization concept by picking and choosing which of its characteristics we want to adopt and which ones we reject, because that approach would weaken it.

There is a certain magic that occurs when you are running business logic on a decentralized consensus layer that is not controlled by any single entity, yet it is jointly owned and operated by several parties who collectively benefit from this arrangement. There is magic when you figure out the blockchain's touch points to your business and you start offering new user experiences that didn't exist before.

These new areas will include banking without banks, gambling without the house's edge, title transfers without central authorities stamping them, e-commerce without eBay, registrations without government officials overseeing them, computer storage without Dropbox, transportation services without Uber, computing without Amazon Web Services, online identities without Google, and that list will continue to grow. Take any services and add "without previous center-based authority," and replace with "peer-to-peer, trust-based network," and you will start to imagine the possibilities.

The general characteristics of decentralization-based services include:

- Speed in settlements
- No intermediary delays
- Upfront identification and reputation
- Flat structure with no overhead
- Permission-less user access
- Trust built inside the network
- Resiliency against attacks
- No censorship
- No central point of failure
- Governance decisions by consensus
- Peer-to-peer communications

THE CRYPTO ECONOMY

What started as Bitcoin, the poster child cryptocurrency that captured our imagination, is leading to a multiplicity of blockchain-enabled businesses and implementations. Going forward, this is metamorphosing into something bigger: a cryptotech-driven economy with unparalleled global value creation opportunities, not unlike the Web's own economy.

Welcome to the crypto economy.

Contrary to what is seemingly visible today, this crypto economy will not be born by attempting to take over the current financial services system, nor by waiting for consumers to transfer their sovereign-backed currency holdings into cryptocurrency wallets. It will emerge by creating its own wealth, validating new types of services and businesses that extend beyond money transactions.

The crypto economy is part of the next phase of the Internet's evolution: the decentralization era.

To understand how cryptocurrency-based blockchain markets can lead us into this new frontier, let us revisit the relationships between money, value, rights, payments, and revenues within the context of cryptocurrency. From there, let us answer two basic questions:

- What is money?
- What is the purpose of money?

Money is a form of value. But not all value is money. We could argue that value has a higher hierarchy than money. In the digital realm, a cryptocurrency is the perfect digital money. The blockchain is a perfect exchange platform for digital value, and it rides on the Internet, the largest connected network on the planet. The resulting combustion is spectacular: digital value that can move fast, freely, efficiently, and cheaply. That is why we have called the blockchain a new "value exchange" network.

The purpose of money is to pay for something that has a value attached to it. Typically, you pay to obtain "rights" for owning or using something.

Cryptocurrency, because of its programmability aspects, embodies digital information that can enable other capabilities. When you "pay" via cryptocurrency, that transaction could include additional trust-related rights, such as for property, information, custody, access, or voting.

Therefore, the blockchain enables a new form of meta-transaction where the *value is represented by what it unlocks at the end of the transaction, not just by an intrinsic monetary value that gets deposited in a static account.* It sounds like a type of stock market functionality that allows the trading of an unlimited number of unregulated value elements, unlike financial securities that are regulated. And, it is more distributed, more decentralized, and more active in the sense that your "wallet" can trigger actions that are directly wired into the real world.

For example, you could start earning cryptocurrency tokens by sharing your automobile driving data via an app (such as La'Zooz for transportation). The next day, you could catch a shared ride with another La'Zooz driver, and the tokens you earned will be automatically deducted to pay for the ride you are taking.

In this case, no real money was exchanged, and no payment was offered. Instead, cryptocurrency was earned passively (by just driving), information rights were given to the driver (that you were a legitimate passenger with a good reputation), other rights were confirmed to you (that the driver was trustworthy), a service was provided (to be driven somewhere), and value was exchanged (cryptocurrency) in combined forms of physical and virtual settings. This is an excellent example in the "difficult" category among blockchain-related applications, because many variables and market conditions need to exist for this whole value exchange ecosystem to work. (This is why the La'Zooz service has not launched yet, almost two years after its initial inception)

Hopefully, we will see additional examples of closed loop value exchange where *you are getting paid to share information that leads to a transaction opportunity.*

La'Zooz is the archetype crypto economy model that creates its own mini-economy with a liquid market of value exchange between producers and consumers. Following the example of this operating model, blockchains can enable the creation of cryptocurrency markets, an important feature that goes beyond and above the blockchain's incomplete depiction of being simply a "distributed ledger."

This will create *new movement choices for value creation*, beyond what traditional currencies enable.

How do we get there? With most enabling technologies, we typically begin by duplicating old habits, often by doing the same processes faster or cheaper. Then we start to innovate by doing things differently, and by applying new ideas that we could not see before. Similarly, the Internet took off as soon as we started to program it with "Web applications," precisely the same path that the crypto-tech revolution is on.

This gets us to the next nugget in this emerging puzzle: *how do we create new value?*

You create value by running services on the blockchain.

Blockchain services will succeed by creating a new ecosystem (just like the Web did), and it will get stronger on its own over time.

There is a precedent to what has already happened in cyberspace. With the Internet, we had e-commerce, e-business, e-services, e-markets, and later the social web arrived in the form of large-scale social networks. Each one of these segments created its own wealth.

Thus far, there is no clear segmentation in the emerging field of "blockchain services," but they will be in the form of services where a trust component is stored on the blockchain (identity, rights, membership, ownership, voting, time stamping, content attribution), services where a contractual component is executed on the blockchain (wagers, family trusts, escrow, proof of work delivery, bounties, proof of bets, proof of compliance), decentralized peer-to-peer marketplaces (such as OpenBazaar or La'Zooz), and Distributed Autonomous Organizations (DAO) whose governance and operations run on the blockchain.

What is common to these blockchain services? They run on a

blockchain, can multiply and grow without central control, and they are fueled by cryptocurrency. The cryptocurrency is like fuel; it's collected in part as toll, in part as earnout by the participating users and those that provide these services. You can start to see how cryptocurrency is generated out of crypto-services to instigate a new economy of wealth creation.

Over time, there will be a critical mass of users with significant cryptocurrency balances in their accounts, and further network effects benefits will ensue. Only then can the crypto economy claim to have made potential dents in the current financial system in contrast to the "one nation-one sovereign currency" paradigm.

A NEW FLOW OF VALUE

The blockchain enables a new "flow of value," a concept related to 2001 Nobel laureate in economics Michael Spence's[5] work on how digital technologies transform global value chains through the dynamics of information flows.

Michael Spence observed that emerging economies were growing at rates not seen before, primarily due to the enabling effect of the larger global economy. He attributed the acceleration in the flow of knowledge, technology and learning, as the main linkage to the acceleration in their growth.

We have a similar situation relating to what the blockchain is enabling. The emergence of a new global crypto economy will have similar growth characteristics as the global economy: it will let its actors participate in large markets, and gain access to knowledge, technology, and know-how.

The blockchain is the latest digital value leveler as it impacts and shifts value within the cryptospace and into our physical spaces. The blockchain moves the power of transactions closer to the individuals, and it empowers any user on earth to align themselves with a decentralized application or organization, and start generating or moving their own nucleus of crypto value. Another benefit of this phenomenon is to put the sharing economy on steroids, as it melds (crypto) capital and labor with mobile, location-agnostic marketplace environments.

We are in the early stages of understanding the movement, distribution and creation of "value" outside of the traditional norms of currency, commodity and property as the main vehicles for value transfer and appreciation. A new frontier will appear.

HOW TECHNOLOGY PERMEATES

Time to look into a crystal ball and predict the future of Bitcoin, blockchains, cryptocurrency, decentralized applications and cryptography-based protocols and platforms. All of this activity is under what I like to call Crypto-Tech, a parallel to Info-Tech, which is everything related to information technology.

At the macro level, the future of Crypto-Tech will unfold in ways that may not be so different from how the Internet unfolded. From an endgame point of view; over the past 20 years, the Internet has generated impact along these four dimensions:

1. New Internet-only companies have emerged, and they introduced new user behaviors.
2. Existing organizations (and governments) have adopted the Internet inside their operations.
3. Some industries were threatened or transformed, as the Internet radically changed or hurt them.
4. Web-based software development became a technology staple for any software application development.

HOW NEW TECHNOLOGY PERMEATES

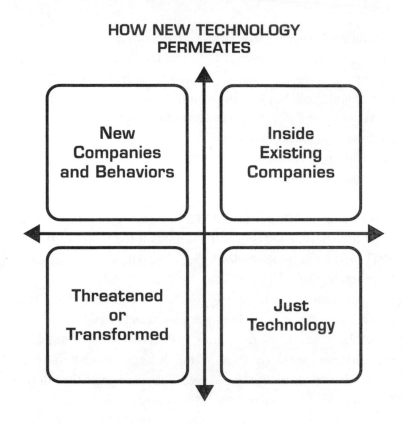

Fast forward 10 years from now, you could replace the word Internet by Crypto-Tech, and the same endgame would hold true: 1) new Crypto-Tech giants will emerge after being start-ups, 2) organizations and governments will adopt new solutions, 3) industries (and some companies) will be threatened and will be affected, and 4) Crypto-Tech development will become part of the software development fabric.

So how will we get there? Let us peer into 2025.

PEERING INTO 2025

There is a long list of predictions for the remainder of this decade and the early parts of the next one. Let us depict the wide range of scenarios that the blockchain will enable.

New Companies & Behaviors

- Online identity and reputation will be decentralized. We will own the data that belongs to us.
- We will self-manage our online reputations, and as we interact with various people or businesses, only the relevant slices of data will be revealed to them.
- Cryptocurrency-only banks will emerge, offering a variety of financial services based on virtual currencies.
- Decentralized prediction markets will enter the mainstream and offer frequent and credible predictions.
- Distributed Autonomous Organizations (DAOs) will become viable, with self-governed operations and user-generated value creation that tie-back directly to services and financial rewards.
- Spontaneous and trusted commerce will happen between peers, without central intermediaries, and with little to no friction.
- Content distribution and attributions will be signed on the blockchain in irrefutable ways.
- Ownership authenticity will be easily verifiable for digital assets and physical products alike.
- Digital or hardware e-wallets will become mainstream, or embedded in smartphones and wearables.
- Seamless micro-transactions will be routine, as easily done as giving tips in real life.
- Registry services for assets will exist and become more routinely done online than by visiting physical authorities.
- Any person will be able to implement business logic and

agreements between other people, and easily enforce them on blockchains.

- Services where users earn cryptocurrency by performing routine services will grow in popularity.
- Blockchains will become large repositories of semi-private information, revealed only when two or more parties agree to disclose it.
- Global remittances will be routinely performed from smartphones or computers, and as easily done as sending an email.
- Users will touch blockchain-based technology without being aware of its existence, just like using databases in the background.
- New decentralized financial clearing networks will challenge existing clearinghouses.
- Digital representations of any physical commodity or asset (as examples: gold, silver, diamonds) will be traded on blockchains, anywhere in the world.
- There will be dozens of commonly used, global virtual currencies that will be considered mainstream, and their total market value will exceed $5 trillion, and represent 5% of the world's $100 trillion economy in 2025.

Inside Existing Companies

- Healthcare medical records will be instantly, securely, and permanently shared between patients and doctors. They will be routinely updated in a decentralized fashion from secure, trusted locations and healthcare providers.
- Legally binding governance-related matters will be easily implemented across distributed teams.
- Remote voting will be trusted, even at national levels, in legally binding political elections.
- Trading exchanges (stocks, commodity, financial instruments) will adopt blockchain-based trust services for validating

transactions, and streamlining their market-clearing activities.

- Most banks will support routine bi-directional crypto-currency transactions (between regular currency and cryptocurrency).
- Most merchants will accept cryptocurrency as a payment option.
- Accounting, billing and financial packages will include cryptocurrency as standard choices, including crypto-equity.
- Digital goods will be invisibly stamped for their origin authenticity, as a routine. Users will be given visibility into global productions by peering into the transparency of supply chains. We will know the utmost provenance details for a variety of products, ensuring their authenticity, quality, and origins are truthfully disclosed.

Threatened or Transformed

- Any business that does not combine its real-world information into a blockchain, just as the Web mirrors and extends an existing business into the online and mobile worlds.
- Clearinghouses with high latency, steep fees, and too much centralization of risk.
- Any broker/dealer that does not offer blockchain-enabled asset value transfers and trades.
- Central lenders that do not evolve how they lend money.
- Banks not adopting crypto-technologies.
- Government services that do not offer even more remote services, such as registries, record keeping, licenses, and identifications.
- Notaries who cannot operate virtually with cryptographically secured documents.
- Anyone who is empowered to issue contracts, signatures, escrows, trusts, certifications, arbitration, trademarks, licenses, ownership proofs, wills, or other private records.

- Decentralized consensus protocols will become a common part of any technology stack implementation, both in public and private settings.
- Commonly used technologies will include Distributed Hash Tables (DHT) and the InterPlanetary File System (IPFS).
- Key-value store databases will be more commonly used.
- Special browsers will enable unique blockchain peering capabilities.
- Smart contract languages will proliferate.
- Writing decentralized applications will become as popular as writing Web apps today.
- Open source protocols will be used and support the creation of new business services and products.
- Running business logic that contains trust and verification components will be plug and play in the practical sense.
- Peer-to-peer decentralized base layers will be common in data storage, computing infrastructure, identity, and reputation.
- Decentralized trust will be relegated to the network and embedded inside the applications instead of controlled by intermediaries.
- University degrees in Cryptography and Game Theory will become popular.
- More decentralized forms of cloud computing will emerge.

This all comes with one warning from a key lesson I learned during the Internet dot-com crash of the year 2000.

Speed kills.

Speed in hyping what the blockchain can do will end-up derailing it, putting us ahead of reality. This type of disconnect is guaranteed to disappoint those who expect benefits faster than what is possible.

That said, keeping with Carlota Perez's[6] model of explaining how technological revolutions unfold, there may be no escaping the fact a crash will happen somewhere between the blockchain's installation phase (2015–2018), and its resulting deployment phase (2018 and beyond). Carlota Perez is a known scholar who researched the concept of techno-economic paradigm shifts and the theory of great surges. This means that, if Carlota Perez is right, we will likely overshoot with exuberance into the installation phase, before smooth sailing into a prosperous deployment phase.

KEY IDEAS FROM CHAPTER SEVEN

1. Blockchains are not just for the enterprise. They also enable decentralization and ultimately, the creation of a new crypto economy, similar to the Web economy which we are familiar with.

2. Getting to decentralization is easier if you start from scratch. It is more difficult to transition from central services to decentralized ones.

3. Crypto economy markets will exist, and they will create their own wealth and economic systems, where participants get paid to provide value that leads to a transaction opportunity.

4. The blockchain enables a new flow of value, enabling the emergence of a global crypto economy, and creating large market opportunities where value is exchanged between the cryptospace and physical spaces.

5. Blockchain technology will permeate our economy, creating new players, threatening others, and forcing change on incumbent organizations that want to survive.

NOTES

1. The Use of Knowledge in Society, F.A. Hayek, http://www.kysq.org/docs/Hayek_45.pdf, 1945.

2. Web We Want, https://webwewant.org.

3. Dodd–Frank Wall Street Reform and Consumer Protection Act, Wikipedia, https://en.wikipedia.org/wiki/Dodd%E2%80%93Frank_Wall_Street_Reform_and_Consumer_Protection_Act.

4. "Stablization Will not Save Us," Nassim Nicholas Taleb, *New York Times*, http://www.nytimes.com/2012/12/24/opinion/stabilization-wont-save-us.html?_r=0.

5. Michael Spence, Wikipedia, https://en.wikipedia.org/wiki/Michael_Spence.

6. Carlota Perez, *Technological Revolutions and Financial Capital: The Dynamics of Bubbles and Golden Ages*, Elgar Online, 2002.

EPILOGUE

BLOCKCHAIN TECHNOLOGY WAS NOT CALLED FOR. It just happened. If you reacted initially, maybe you have a head start. If you didn't, perhaps you can shift a gear, and become proactive. Whether you are leading or following, eventually you will have to sharpen your blockchain strategy.

Implementing the blockchain is still a new competency. The uncertainties, however, cannot be used as an excuse to hold up what must be done. All of us engaged are pioneers on a journey, and we have a responsibility to keep sharing what we are learning, so we can keep lighting the way for those that are behind us. It may take us longer to arrive at our destinations, but it will certainly help the followers, and they will pay us back by making the market bigger and easier to navigate. The future success of blockchains will depend critically on hundreds of millions of people using them.

Blockchains are more than business-technology enablers. They are instruments of social and political change. If we miss their higher calling, we would be falling short of realizing their fullest potential.

One valuable blockchain outcome we exposed is the emergent crypto economy, the sum of the economic realizations resulting from applying the blockchain's potential. This crypto economy is a trust economy that is decentralized at birth, both politically and architecturally; and it lends equal access and lower barriers of entry to all. As we prepare to get on board the crypto economy, undoubtedly it looks fuzzy, foggy, buggy, risky, uncertain, and unproven. Then suddenly, it will blossom and grow with more benefits than disadvantages.

Although we have explored the blockchain topic at length in this book, we have certainly not exhausted everything to be explored. There is plenty more that will unfold, much of it from your own discoveries. I am sure that the best cases and ideas are not yet in the blockchain wild. Still, there remains many unanswered questions. What will be the impact of blockchains on the world economy? Who will be the Amazons, Googles, and Facebooks of the blockchain? What will be the tipping point? Will regulators stay patient, or will they prematurely declare their intentions? If the consensus ledger is the hammer, can we also find the nail?

The blockchain's message is simple, but strong. Let innovation lead. The blockchain is not about a better Web, a better bank, or a better service. The survival of the blockchain will depend on what you will do with it, and it is not only about its technical features. Its adoption will be gradual, starting with developers and startup entrepreneurs, then techno-business people, followed by organizations that see change, and society demanding change, and ending with organizations that once resisted change.

Amidst this activity lies a dichotomy of hope. Startups are inherently optimistic, and enterprises are sometimes skeptical. As a result of blockchain-enabled business models, some existing intermediaries will be at risk. We know it. And some new ones will emerge, perhaps more as virtual, transparent, and distributed entities that can be trusted programmatically.

My wish is *The Business Blockchain* has in some way inspired and guided you. If you enjoyed it, I invite you to explore further how to rethink trust, wealth, and information in my next book, *Centerless*. The new era of decentralization will soon be upon us.

Blockchains do not impose restrictions on us. To the opposite, they grant us new levels of freedom, and let us program our world on top of them, any way we would like.

Blockchains will be the best new tool of the decade.

SELECTED BIBLIOGRAPHY

Buterin, Vitalik. "Ethereum and Oracles." *Ethereum Blog*. 2014.
https://blog.ethereum.org/2014/07/22/ethereum-and-oracles/.

Chaum, David, Debajyoti Das, Aniket Kate, Farid Javani, Alan
T. Sherman, Anna Krasnova, and Joeri de Ruiter. "cMix:
Anonymization by High-Performance Scalable Mixing." *Cryptology
ePrint Archive*. 2016. http://eprint.iacr.org/2016/008.pdf.

Chaum, David. "Anniversary Keynote Address Speech, Financial
Cryptography and Data Security 2016." *Twentieth International
Conference*. February 22–26, 2016.

"Elements Project, Blockstream." *GitHub*. 2015. https://github.com/
ElementsProject.

"Embracing Disruption: Embracing Disruption: Tapping the Potential of
Distributed Kedgers to Improve the Post-trade Landscape." *DTCC*.
January 2016.

Giancarlo, J. Christopher. "Regulators and the Blockchain: First, Do No
Harm." *Special Address of CFTC Commissioner Before the Depository
Trust & Clearing Corporation*. Blockchain Symposium. March 29, 2016.

Hammer, Michael, and James Champy. *Reengineering the Corporation: A
Manifesto for Business Revolution*. New York: HarperCollins, 1993.

Kelly, Kevin. *Out of Control: The New Biology of Machines, Social
Systems, & the Economic World*. New York: Basic Books, 1995.

Mougayar, William, and David Cohen. "After the Social Web, Here
Comes the Trust Web." *TechCrunch*. 2015.
http://startupmanagement.org/2014/04/10the-bitcoin-and-
cryptocurrency-investment-landscape/.

Mougayar, William. *Opening Digital Markets: Battle Plans and Business Strategies for Internet Commerce.* New York: McGraw-Hill, 1997.

———. "How the Cryptoconomy Will Be Created." *Forbes.* 2015. http://www.forbes.com/sites/valleyvoices/2015/01/20/how-the-cryptoconomy-will-be-created/#388906916787.

———. "Understanding the Blockchain." *O'Reilly Radar.* 2015. https://www.oreilly.com/ideas/understanding-the-blockchain.

———. "Why The Blockchain Is the New Website." *Forbes.* 2015. http://www.forbes.com/sites/valleyvoices/2015/12/21/why-the-blockchain-is-the-new-website/#9292bb1ac2ef.

———. "The Bitcoin and Cryptocurrency Investment Landscape." *Startup Management.* 2014. http://startupmanagement.org/2014/04/10/the-bitcoin-and-cryptocurrency-investment-landscape/.

———. "An Operational Framework for Decentralized Autonomous Organizations." *Startup Management.* 2015. http://startupmanagement.org/2015/02/04/an-operational-framework-for-decentralized-autonomous-organizations/.

"Open Blockchain Whitepaper." *IBM.* 2016. https://github.com/openblockchain/obc-docs/blob/master/whitepaper.md.

Stanek, Dušan, Marián Vrabko, Markéta Selucká, Vladislav Mičátek, and Robert Siuciński. *A Lawyer's Introduction to Smart Contracts.* Łask, Scientia Nobilitat, 2014.

Swanson, Tim. *Great Chain of Numbers: A Guide to Smart Contracts, Smart Property and Trustless Asset Management.* Amazon Digital Services, 2014.

Thomas, Stefan, and Evan Schwartz. "Smart Oracles: A Simple, Powerful Approach to Smart Contracts." *Codius.* 2014. https://github.com/codius/codius/wiki/.

Toffler, Alvin. *Powershift: Knowledge, Wealth, and Violence at the Edge of the 21st Century.* New York: Bantam Books, 1991.

INDEX

ADDITIONAL RESOURCES

Executive Presentations by William Mougayar, Explaining the
Impact of the Blockchain and Decentralization
As a trained professional consultant and analyst, William starts
by understanding the context and unique requirements of each
audience he addresses. He typically complements his delivery with
pertinent insights that are the result of understanding your objectives and your particular situation.

For conference keynotes, or private briefings with corporate executives, please contact *speaking@vcapv.com.*

The Business Blockchain Book Site
THEBUSINESSBLOCKCHAIN.COM
Follow and sign up for updates, new research, and events pertain-
ing to *The Business Blockchain.*

Startup Management
STARTUPMANAGEMENT.ORG
A library of over 2,000 curated articles on growing, scaling, and
managing startups; syndicated into the Harvard Business School
Entrepreneurship Insights website at the Arthur Rock Center for
Entrepreneurship.

William's Blog

STARTUPMANAGEMENT.ORG/BLOG

A must-read, to follow William's ongoing thoughts, updates to his popular industry landscape, and research on the blockchain, decentralization, and tech startups.

OnBlockchains Super Aggregator

ONBLOCKCHAINS.ORG

Super news aggregator on the blockchain and cryptocurrencies. It publishes over 300 pieces of content daily from about 180 feeds. Most concentrated single feed of news on the blockchain.

Virtual Capital Ventures

VCAPV.COM

Virtual Capital Ventures is a boutique style, early stage technology venture fund, based in Toronto. VcapV's thesis is to invest in openly decentralized, networked applications and technologies that reimagine industries and sectors through the creation of new intermediaries or protocols.

ABOUT THE AUTHOR

WILLIAM MOUGAYAR is a general partner at Virtual Capital Ventures, a boutique style, early-stage technology venture capital firm, focused on decentralized technologies and applications. Based in Toronto, the VcapV fund is advised and backed by some of the industry's top players.

William is on the board of directors of OB1, the OpenBazaar open source protocol that is pioneering decentralized peer-to-peer commerce; a special board advisor to the Ethereum Foundation, the leading blockchain technology platform for decentralized applications; a member of OMERS Ventures Board of Advisors, one of Canada's top venture capital firms; an advisory board member to the Coin Center, the Washington DC-based leading non-profit research and advocacy center focused on the public policy issues facing cryptocurrency technologies, a board advisor to Bloq, founder of Startup Management, and Techstars mentor.

In the early Internet years, he was the founding chairman of CommerceNet Canada, and authored two books, *Opening Digital Markets* (McGraw-Hill, 1997), and *The Business Internet and Intranets* (Harvard Business School Press, 1997).

William started and raised money for three companies (two of them were sold), Engagio, Eqentia, and CYBERManagement. His career includes 14 years at Hewlett-Packard in senior sales and marketing management roles, 10 years as an independent management consultant and thought leader, and three years as global vice president of corporate marketing at Cognizant in Teaneck, New Jersey. In 2005, he was vice president, IT practice at Aberdeen Group in Boston. Over the years, he has consulted to numerous Fortune 500 companies, and is a professional speaker.

William is a graduate of the University of Washington, the University of Western Ontario Ivey School of Business, and attended the University of British Columbia Graduate Commerce School.

Email: wmougayar@gmail.com

Twitter: @wmougayar